God in My Life

3

Rita Kay Crowder Roberts

World rights reserved. This book or any portion thereof may not be copied or reproduced in any form or manner whatever, except as provided by law, without the written permission of the publisher, except by a reviewer who may quote brief passages in a review.

The author assumes full responsibility for the accuracy of all facts and quotations as cited in this book. The opinions expressed in this book are the author's personal views and interpretations, and do not necessarily reflect those of the publisher.

This book is provided with the understanding that the publisher is not engaged in giving spiritual, legal, medical, or other professional advice. If authoritative advice is needed, the reader should seek the counsel of a competent professional. All Bible references are taken from the King James Version (KJV) of the Bible. Public domain.

Copyright © 2025 Rita Kay Crowder Roberts
Copyright © 2025 TEACH Services, Inc.
ISBN-13: 978-1-4796-1679-4 (Paperback)
ISBN-13: 978-1-4796-1680-0 (ePub)
Library of Congress Control Number: 2024910533

Dedication

I dedicate this book and my whole life to Jesus, the Son of God. Jesus is the King in my life. He is my best Friend, my Maker, my Counselor, my Judge, my Defender, my Protector, and my Savior.

Thank you, heavenly Father, for Your Son, for Your love and patience with me, and Your amazing grace for me. Without You, I can do nothing, and without You I am nothing!

A Word of Thanks to ...

Penney Morton Smith

Dallas and Susanna Roberts

Atsushi and Katy (Roberts) Yamamuro

Jacobus and Rachel Roberts Fourie

Diana Roberts

Daniel Roberts

Katie Rives

... and to everyone who donated help and information, and for all their time, work, and encouragement with this book.

.

Table of Contents

Prologue ix
God in My Life 1
Song: "God Took Care of the Baby" 5
The Deception 6
The Apartment 11
Song: "Throw Out the Life-Line" 14
The Boxes 15
The Illness 18
Song: "God Will Take Care of You" 21
The Influence 22
Song: "Bring Them In" 25
The "Somebody" 26
The Stick Horse 28
The Mud 31
The Sled 34
The Cake 37
The Arm 41
Song: "Does Jesus Care?" 43
The Move 44
Song: "Doing My Best" 46
The Friend 47
The Dresses 50
Song: "Long Ago in Old Judea" 52

The Dream 53
The Dent 56
The Rooms 58
Song: "Jesus Bids Us Shine" 63
The Table 64
The Flirt 66
Song: "Make Me a Blessing" 72
The Addiction 73
The Cookies 80
The Knot 84
The Diet 86
Song: "O Love That Wilt Not Let Me Go" 92
The Neatness Lesson 93
The Law 95
Song: "The Lord's Commands" 102
Song: "The Bible Stands" 103
The Return 104
Song: "Look for the Waymarks" 109
Song: "'Tis Almost Time for the Lord to Come" 110
Song: "Jesus Is Coming Again" 111
The Power of Our Awesome God 112
Epilogue 119
Song: "Hold the Fort" 120
Bibliography 121

Prologue

If you have read either of the first two books in this series, GOD IN MY LIFE, then you know why I use the word AWESOME only for God. It is the best word that we have in the English language to describe God, so I use it only for Him in these books.

God bless you, dear friend, as you read these miracles and know that God is in YOUR life too! Talk to Him just like you do to your human friends—and see for yourself that **when prayer becomes a habit, then miracles become a lifestyle.**

God in My Life

Society and our lifestyle nowadays have us super busy. Busy with schedules, our own, plusBig everybody else's. Do we even think, "Is God in **my life**?" *IS* God in our lives?

When I am taking the stairs five at a time to save time instead of waiting for the elevator, because I'm already ten minutes late to my yearly interview with the head boss, is God there somewhere?

When I'm driving ninety mph in a thirty-five-mph zone to get my kids to school in three minutes, is God around somewhere?

Rush, more rush—who has time to think about God? Do you suppose God is too busy to think about me/us too? I wonder?

I used to rush so much—I'd catch myself saying, "Thank You, God, for helping me with that problem **yesterday**." Or "God, remind me to talk to You tonight, when I have more time." Or not even talking to Him at all for days. During that time, even though I wasn't thinking about Him or talking to Him, do you suppose He was thinking about me, watching me, or even caring about me at all?

My first recollection of anything in my life isn't really from my memory. It is a story my mother told me.

God was even in my life's first encounter. All babies are miracles. God is always there when we are born. Plus, He's the one that gives them the initial push to start them down the birth canal. So, of course He is there. It's a good thing, too, that He's there. I don't know how else I would have been able to handle the delivery room experience alone when I was born, being one so young and terribly inexperienced.

Just before my grand appearance in the delivery room, the attending nurse, in her rush to get ready for my delivery, dropped and broke the ether bottle (they used to use ether back then) spilling the contents across the whole floor. The stupefying odor wafted up into the nostrils of everyone present. Having to continue breathing, the doctor, nurses, and my parents inhaled the sleep-inducing odor. My daddy must have breathed in way too much of the ether, because in all the excitement and panic, he fainted on to the floor, which added to the concern and worry of the now very sluggish doctor and nurses. Not to say anything about my dear mother trying to stay awake enough to "push." The whole group in the delivery room would have gone to sleep, missing my grand entry totally, had it not been for the fact that the room was "old-fashioned" and had an outside window. The same nurse, finally thinking of this, raised the window, letting in precious fresh air, and allowing the previous room aroma to escape. This revived the whole delivery room party, and they were able to continue escorting me into God's world.

I'm certainly thankful to God for making the fresh air for me and for you too.

I'm glad God was there then and gave that nurse presence of mind to open the window in time or I, too, probably would have gone to sleep and slept through the "grand entry" episode, making it necessary to eliminate the "grand" part.

Even writing these books, God is here in it. A few years ago, a recipient of my yearly letters—I would try to write my family and friends and keep in touch with them as much as possible, which turns out to be not as often I would like—came up to me at camp meeting and said, "You should be a writer." Of course, I laughed. But God kept working on me to do just that.

Finally, one day, I said to Him, "OK! OK! I'll write. But what will I write?"

Immediately, "how God has guided your life" came to my mind.

"No," I argued, "that's what everyone is writing about."

"But they are not writing about God in **your life**," came the reply. "They are writing about God in **their** life," was the answer that came back to me.

Then, of all things, that next Sabbath, in our Sabbath School class, the teacher was reminding us to use what God has given us for Him. And someone spoke up and told how, when she first learned the truth, she was convicted that the seventh-day Sabbath was the right day to keep. So, she told God, just as soon as she got her fifteen-year-old son raised, and all the things that needed to be done to help her husband, then she would start obeying God's law totally. But right now, she was too busy and had to tend to her husband and son first. Her son died that next February, and her husband died six months later in August. She told us that she then realized how important it is to obey God immediately when you learn what truth is and what He wants you to do.

My eyes were watering when she finished her story, because I too realized that nothing, absolutely nothing, should come between me and God or keep me from obeying Him. I wasn't sure why He wanted me to write these books, and He was going to have to tell me what to write, but I had to be willing to let Him use me at all times and quit being too busy to listen to Him and to obey Him.

In the process of teaching all of this to me, God gave me this poem some years ago:

WHOSE TIME IS IT?

I haven't time for anything,
I'm busy as can be,
I have to meet my schedules
There's many—can't you see?

There's hurry here and hurry there,
The rush—it will not end.
I haven't time to pray—dear Lord.
There's no time with Thee, to spend.

Yes, I know that child needs guiding.
But my time is set, you see.
Surely, someone else will do it,
Someone, instead of busy me.

Then there's the elderly one needing comfort.
Dear me, Lord, there's bound to be
Someone else with much more time,
Much, much more—than me.

Oh, there's someone asking questions
About my Bible, what do I believe?
They can surely ask a preacher,
He will know what I believe.

My neighbor is discouraged.
But what is that to me?
My time is much more valuable,
I hope that they can see.
And I'm still young, Lord.
Life is still ahead.
Can't the older ones do Your bidding?
They surely have more time instead.

Lord, what are You saying?
You, have given me—my time—
Time for loving, caring, sharing.
All for Thee—Thy time—sublime.

But, Lord, my time is so important.
I have so many things to do.
My <u>life</u> is so important.
Each day is something new.

Busy, busy, all the time.
Appointments that need keeping.
And I haven't any time
For those who are really seeking.

Lord, why do You turn Your back?
I'm still talking, can't You see?
Look back at me, Lord,
Please, look back at me!

Too late, I see.
That time You gave me, Lord,
That time was meant for Thee.

By Rita Roberts

The Deception

In the chapter entitled, "My Friend Mildred" of *GOD IN MY LIFE*, book 2, we already learned some of the Bible verses showing us how Satan and his demon angels can impersonate dead people and pretend to be our dead friends and/or relatives who have come back to life to tell us something. But what about Satan and his demons and angels impersonating people who are still alive? Can and will he try to deceive us by pretending to be someone who is still alive?

The answer is yes!

I grew up mostly in Orlando, Florida, and we would spend a few weeks of the summers in the mountains of Fletcher, North Carolina, with my grandmother Lela, aunts, uncles, and cousins. Oh, what fun! After we got to North Carolina the summer I turned ten years old, my mother, Kate, received a letter from our friends in Orlando, stating that they would be coming through our mountain area in a couple of weeks and wanted to stop and see us. We were delighted! Mother gave them directions to Grandma's house. Two weeks later, on Tuesday, the designated day, my good friend Gail and her family showed up at 10:00 in the morning.

Gail and I were such good friends and got along so well together; we were so happy to get together this time. We were about the same age and height. We both had long blonde hair and both wore it in a ponytail most of the time. Sometimes people thought we were sisters. Gail, her oldest sister, younger brother, and I all had a good time together. Some of my cousins that lived close by came over and we all played and had so much fun while the adults visited.

Hours later, after Grandma's good meal, Gail and her family had to leave to continue their trip on to Michigan. It was sad to see them go, but we were so thankful that they had come, even for that short time.

The next morning, Wednesday, at 10:00, I was out on Grandma's front porch playing, when I heard the most horrible racket—deafening cars, like the loud sound of all the cars together racing by you in a car race on the racetrack.

I turned and looked toward the road but did not see anything at first. The loud noise was coming from the road out in front of the house but was to the left, above the driveway, on the other side of the trees where I could not see. As I stood there watching, I saw Gail's blue car come racing down the road, past our house; her mother was driving, her sister was on the passenger side of the front seat. Gail and her brother were in the backseat. Her brother was behind their mother and Gail was on the passenger side toward me with her window totally down, and her head out the window, resting on her arms, facing the way they were all going, and her ponytail flying. I cupped my hands around my mouth and yelled as loud as I could, "GAIL!" trying to get her to see me and stop. I was so sure that that was them, and I thought they didn't know they were lost and going by our house again. *If I could just stop them*, I thought, *we could help them find their way back to the main road*. But she did not look. They just kept going.

The car raced by our house very fast to the next curve in the road, which was behind some more trees, so I could not see it again at this point. But there the loud noise stopped, and the car did not go on down the road. I kept watching for it past that curve where you could see the road again, but it never went on down.

Quickly, I ran into the house, yelling, "Mommy, Mommy! Gail and her family are lost! They are still here—they drove by our house going really fast. They didn't even know they are still in North Carolina and that they just drove by our house."

My mother and grandma ran out the front door and looked down the road. But no Gail, no car of any kind, and no car sounds. Only the tweeting and chirping of the Carolina birds.

Mother looked at me as she said, "No, honey, Gail, her mommy, and all are probably in another state by now." She gave me a loving pat on the shoulder, and she and Grandma went back into the house.

Of course, we didn't have any way back then to find out where they were the next day after they left our house, until we all got back to Florida at the end of the summer. We did not have cell phones back then.

After we all got back to Florida, Mother asked Gail's mother, "Where were you at 10:00 the next morning after you left us?"

Gail's mother said, "We were in Kentucky by then."

After learning that, I knew the car and people that I had seen and heard on Wednesday at 10:00 in the morning could not possibly have been our friends.

So, then, who was it?

Then, many, many years later, when my son was in his late teens, and going to our community college, one of his childhood friends was living with us at the time. Dallas and his friend Jon were sleeping in twin beds in the new bedroom that Dallas and his dad had built.

As my children grew up, to awaken them in the morning to get them up and ready for school, I always sat on the side of their bed or stood beside their bed in the dark and gently rubbed their back, singing or talking quietly to them, so they could awaken peacefully, not with bright lights and noise. So, I continue this practice as they were still at home even though they were grown up.

On this particular morning, I was supposed to wake up Dallas at a certain time to get ready to go to his college classes. As usual, I quietly opened his door and tiptoed softly across the room, so as not to awaken Jon. I sat down on the side of Dallas's bed and started massaging his back, saying softly, "Good morning. Did you sleep well?" Usually, as he awakened, his voice was soft and sleepy sounding, answering, "Good morning. Thank you." But this morning his voice was deep, louder, and wide awake, as he said, "You already did that."

I said, "What do you mean?"

He said, "A while ago, you opened the door, walked across the room, sat down here on my bed, started rubbing my back, and talked in your same voice to me."

Of course, that was NOT me. This was the first time I had been in his room that morning. I had been in another part of the house, getting up and getting ready in my own bedroom, and fixing breakfast in the kitchen before time to wake Dallas up. So, whatever, or whoever he was talking about was NOT me.

So, who was it?

As I read my Bible and learn more and more of the truth in the Bible, I realize these kinds of incidences are really Satan's angels and even Satan himself trying to trick and deceive us into believing a lie, something that is NOT true.

If you or I believe it, then Satan can have the same impersonation tell us anything, which would be any kind of lies. In other words, for example, if he impersonates your sibling, and you do not check it out and read your Bible, but assume it is really your sibling, then Satan can use their disguise again and again or even other people to lead you astray. Satan can use anyone and anything to deceive any of us. Only our trust and knowledge of God through prayer and His Word can keep us from being deceived.

Satan's goal is to make us, you and me, go against what God's Word, the Bible, says.

"[I]n the latter times some shall depart from the faith, giving heed to seducing spirits, and doctrines of devils" (1 Tim. 4:1).

> Satan has his allies in men. And evil angels in human form will appear to men, and present before them such glowing representations of what they will be able to do if they will only heed their suggestions, that often they change their penitence for defiance.... Sin has darkened the reasoning powers, and hell is triumphing. O, will not men cease to trust in human beings? (*Testimonies for the Church Containing Messages of Warning and Instruction to Seventh-day Adventists,* p. 21)

> Satan will use every opportunity to seduce men from their allegiance to God. He and the angels who fell with him will appear on the earth as men, seeking to deceive.... Evil angels in the form of men will talk with those who know the truth. They will misinterpret and misconstrue the statements of the messengers of God.... Have [we] forgotten the warning given in the sixth chapter of Ephesians? We are engaged in a warfare against the hosts of darkness. Unless we follow our Leader [Jesus] closely, Satan will obtain the victory over us.... Evil angels in the form of believers will work in our ranks to bring in a strong spirit of unbelief. Let not even this discourage you, but bring a true heart to the help of the Lord against the powers of satanic agencies. These powers of evil will assemble in our meetings, not to receive a blessing, but to counterwork the influences of the Spirit of God. (*Last Day Events*, p. 160–161)

"Satanic agencies in human form will take part in this last great conflict to oppose the building up of the kingdom of God.... Satanic agencies are in every city. We cannot afford to be off our guard for one moment" (*Selected Messages*, book 2, p. 383).

Remember, dear reader friend, Satan is lost, and he is trying to pull all of us down with him. His destiny was sealed when he caused the people to kill Jesus on the cross. Ever since he was jealous of Jesus in heaven, Satan has hated Jesus and tried to get at Him. So, since Lucifer (now Satan) could not keep Jesus dead, he is trying to get back at Jesus by getting all the people of the world to sin (breaking and going against God's law) and not be repentant (be sorry), turn away from Jesus, and be lost. Satan

> *Pray every day, you and I, that we will not be deceived by Satan's lies and counterfeits. God loves each one and all of us and wants us saved in His kingdom. God will not let us be deceived if we love Him and totally obey Him.*

knows this will hurt Jesus the most, to lose His people to sin and Satan.

All of the people of the world, including you and me, Jesus loves dearly. He even died for us to give us another opportunity to repent, to be sorry for our sins, to try not to do that sin again, and come back to Him to live with Him forever!

Satan knows how bad it hurts Jesus (and God, His and our Father) to see just one of His people turn against Him and choose to be lost.

Let's pray every day, you and I, that we will not be deceived by Satan's lies and counterfeits. God loves each one and all of us and wants us saved in His kingdom. God will not let us be deceived if we love Him and totally obey Him.

The Apartment

We had just moved into an apartment on the first floor of a large, really nice 200+ apartment complex in Sacramento, California. Our son, Dallas, had his second birthday while we were there. My husband had accepted a job with a company, hanging overhead commercial doors, so was gone during the day.

In this apartment, we had a small patio through a sliding glass door of the living room. The patio was about 6 feet x 10 feet and had high walls, so we could not see over it and other people could not see in. There was a driveway and a parking lot all around the outside of our patio, so we could hear the street noise of the city life, the car horns, the motor noise, and people talking and yelling.

Early one morning, Dallas, who had lived in the country before, and loved to watch the birds feeding in the birdfeeders and listen to them chirping in the trees, came in from the noisy sounds out on the patio, crying his little eyes out, and said through his tears, "Mommy, I can't hear the birdies singing."

I thought right then that as soon as we could arrange it, we needed to move back to the country again. Bless his heart, he sure missed the country life.

Soon after that, one day a pretty cat adopted us. She was white with tan spots. She could easily jump over the patio wall and come in for her daily bowl of milk and to play with Dallas. He just loved her! One day, I found kitty drinking her milk out of her bowl on the patio, and Dallas was bent over her with a spoon in his hand, saying "Kitty, spoon, Kitty, spoon, Kitty, SPOON!" Trying to get her to "eat her milk" with the spoon, since he was learning to eat with a spoon himself.

Kitty came into the apartment, and they played so good together. Just before evening came, she would jump the wall of the patio, and go home (I guess). Then she would come back the next day. I know God had arranged that bit of nature for little Dallas since he missed the animals and birds in the country SO MUCH.

One day, when my husband was on his way to an overhead door job, he passed a really nice park, so the next weekend, he took Dallas and me to see it. It turns out the park was only two blocks from our apartment. The park had swings, slides, teeter-totters, a jungle gym, and all kinds of equipment to play on, and even a sandbox full of sand to play in. Plus, it was close enough that we could walk to it, since my husband had to take our only vehicle to work. Dallas and I loved to go to that park to play every chance we got, whenever the weather was not too hot. When it was 125° and above, it became too hard to breathe walking that far, so we found other things to do in our air-conditioned apartment.

It is in this park that we met Sherilee and her little boy, Bobby. Dallas and Bobby were the same age and played together. Sherilee and I got to be good friends. She and Bobby would come over to our apartment and eat with us; and Dallas and I would visit with them in their home periodically too. God led in our friendship. We spent lots of time talking and being together.

Sherilee had gotten distraught with her church and quit going. One day she told me the story about it all. She said she grew up knowing all about St. Christopher and how he protected her and her family and everyone from accidents and everything pertaining to the car and travel. She felt very secure knowing that the image glued to the middle of the dashboard of their car was her protection. Then all of a sudden, when she was thirteen years old, her church decided to do away with that "saint." Her dad ripped the image of St. Christopher off the dashboard in the car. It left a scar in the paint. Sherilee said, from that moment on to adulthood, she was scared to get into the car, afraid that without St. Christopher they would wreck and be killed. When she got to be an adult, she realized that through all those years her family had been in many cars and driven many miles without St. Christopher's "protection." That's when she realized that it is really the God in heaven that had protected her and her family through all of her growing up years and even now into her adult life. So, from that point on she believed in the God in heaven, not saints (people) and definitely not images of people who have died that couldn't even hear or see.

She told me, "That is so silly of us to believe all that stuff about something protecting us that's not even alive and can't see or hear us, when we already have a living, heavenly Father that <u>really</u> does protect us."

> For the living know that they shall die: but the dead know not any thing, neither have they any more a reward; for the memory of them

is forgotten. Also their love, and their hatred, and their envy, is now perished; neither have they any more a portion for ever in any thing that is done under the sun.… Whatsoever thy hand findeth to do, do it with thy might; for there is no work, nor device, nor knowledge, nor wisdom, in the grave, whither thou goest. (Eccles. 9:5–6, 10)

The idols of the heathen are silver and gold, the work of men's hands. They have mouths, but they speak not; eyes have they, but they see not; they have ears, but they hear not; neither is there any breath in their mouths. They that make them are like unto them: so is every one that trusteth in them. (Ps. 135:15–18)

What profiteth the graven image that the maker thereof hath graven it; the molten image, and a teacher of lies, that the maker of his work trusteth therein, to make dumb [cannot speak] idols? Woe unto him that saith to the wood, Awake; to the dumb stone, Arise, it shall teach! Behold, it is laid over with gold and silver, and there is no breath at all in the midst of it. But the LORD is in his holy temple: let all the earth keep silence before him. (Hab. 2:18–20)

"Ye know that ye were Gentiles, carried away unto these dumb [cannot speak] idols, even as ye were led" (1 Cor. 12:2).

The Boxes

As I said, when my son Dallas was two years old, we had recently moved to the first floor of a large apartment complex in Sacramento, California.

One day, Dallas came into the kitchen where I was busily working, and asked, "Mommy, can I have a box?"

"What kind of box?" I asked.

"A BIG box." Was his reply.

Without further questions, I went to the hall closet, took out one of our packing boxes, and gave it to him. Happily, he took it, went into his room, and closed the door.

Having just finished unpacking from our move to Sacramento, we still had a few empty boxes.

Sometime later, little Dallas returned to ask for another box. Although still busy in the kitchen, I went to get another box from the closet and handed it to him. Again, he took it to his room and closed the door.

A half hour or so later, he emerged from his room with the same request.

I remember thinking, *Why in the world does he want so many boxes?* But still my mind was on my own project in the kitchen, and I didn't think any further of his box needs. I just automatically handed a box to him and went on working.

Still later, he asked one more time for another box.

After a while, my little Dallas walked out of his room, excitedly rubbing his hands together like you do when you have successfully finished a good job, saying, "Well, I'm all ready to go."

Startled, I stopped my busyness, turned toward him, and said quickly, "Ready to go WHERE?"

Since we had just finished unpacking after our move from Los Angeles, we were definitely NOT planning to move again.

With his excitement and beautiful smile, he answered, "Heaven, of course!"

Bless his little heart—the Sabbath before this, in his little cradle roll class at church, his teacher had excitedly told the children that "Jesus is coming soon, and we should be getting ready now to go to heaven with Him."

> *I quickly went into his room, and there on his bed and on the floor were those four boxes, loaded with all his stuffed animals and toys.*

I quickly went into his room, and there on his bed and on the floor were those four boxes, loaded with all his stuffed animals and toys.

One box had only two of his bigger stuffed animals; a couple boxes were overflowing and could not be closed, but one box was even closed. They contained no clothes or things he might REALLY need if moving. But it didn't matter—this little boy was preparing, and in his precious little mind, was all ready to go to heaven.

I didn't have the heart to tell him that we wouldn't be taking our "toys," or anything at all, with us, only our characters.

I was so very proud of my little boy. I praised him for doing his best to be ready for heaven.

I waited until he was taking his nap later that day to unpack and put away his toys, and I put the boxes back into the closet, so they would not remind him of his hard work and make him feel bad.

MY mind worked on me: "Am I, MYSELF, ready for Jesus to come?"

Of course, I know that when Jesus comes, we will not be taking our possessions to heaven. The only thing we will take is our character—our actions and the way we think.

That's why now, instead of thinking of ourselves, we need to be thinking of Jesus: how can we be more like Him? How can we honor Him?

And thinking of other people: how can I help other people see Jesus and His love for them? How can I help other people better their lives?

Am I TRULY ready for Jesus to come?

How about you, dear friend? Are you TRULY ready for Jesus to come?

In Jesus' own words: "Verily I say unto you, Except ye be converted, and become as little children, ye shall not enter into the kingdom of heaven" (Matt. 18:3).

The Illness

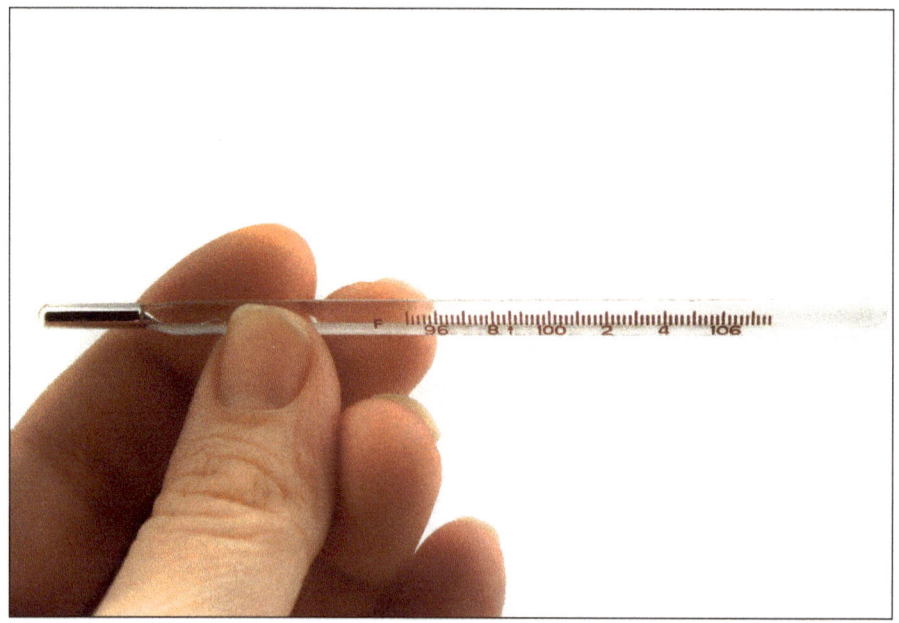

While we lived in that same apartment in Sacramento, California, our two-year-old Dallas got very sick. We had just moved from an area in Los Angeles where there was smog. The triplex houses there were about four or five feet apart with a narrow walkway between them. On some days, the smog was so thick that I could not even see the triplex right next door.

I believe, that possibly, the smog that collected in his little lungs might have contributed to whatever illness my little boy had.

After we arrived in Sacramento, Dallas's neck swelled up to the size of his head; that white "sleep" like kind of pus started pouring out of his eyes and down his cheeks; also, his temperature ran over 104° every night; then in the morning it would drop to 100° but never lower than that. Then worked back up to 104–105° throughout the day. Little Dallas cried and cried a lot, even sometimes while I was holding him.

I took him to the first recommended doctor; even the doctor could not figure out what the illness was, but he wrote out a prescription anyway. In desperation I filled it and started giving my little two year old drugs (giving him drugs just tore me up).

Yet Dallas was still sick.

So, I took him to another recommended doctor. He too, could not figure out what it was but wrote out another prescription.

I filled it and gave it to him however many times a day the directions said. But no change. Dallas still didn't get better.

By now, I did not know where else to ask about doctors, so I was picking them out of the phone book myself. Of course, we did not have Internet back then in which to look things up. This all went on without Dallas getting any better for nine weeks. Our little boy was so very sick.

I thought at first that it was mumps, with his large neck. But **ALL** of the eight doctors (yes, we ended up going to eight doctors) said it was **NOT** mumps, but none of them knew **WHAT** it really was.

By this time there were eight bottles of medicines that my little boy was taking at different times of the day. Besides all that horrible poison going into his little body, we had paid $50 to $75 for each of those bottles of medicine.

My very sick little son could only sleep for fifteen-minute intervals at night, when I wasn't holding him. He would wake up after fifteen minutes and cry, so I held him most of the day and night. He and I were both exhausted.

So, I got back down on my knees (for the umpteenth time) beside my bed, in front of my unopened suitcase, bowed my head, closed my eyes, clasped my hands together, and begged earnestly and for the first time this way, "God please show me what to do to help my little boy get well."

One Thursday evening, just after he had gone to sleep for his fifteen-minute sleep; in desperation I got my suitcase out of the closet and laid it on my bed. I decided to pack, take my little boy, and go back home to North Carolina where we already had our trustworthy doctors.

But just as I was about to open my suitcase, I had the strongest "impression" to pray again. Of course, I had been praying this whole nine weeks that God would heal my little boy.

But this time the "strong impression" was "pray again, only this time, pray that God will show **YOU** what to do for Dallas."

So, I got back down on my knees (for the umpteenth time) beside my bed, in front of my unopened suitcase, bowed my head, closed my eyes, clasped my hands together, and begged earnestly and for the first time this way, "God please show me what to do to help my little boy get well."

Instantly God put into my head: "hydrotherapy." My grandmothers and my mother used it for healing most everything. My mother, Kate, always treated my childhood illnesses with it, and I always got well.

But for some reason, this whole nine weeks I had not thought of hydrotherapy (Water treatments). As soon as God said, "hydrotherapy," I prayed, "Thank you, dear God in heaven." I jumped up from my knees, ran into the kitchen, took all those eight bottles of medicine ($400 to $600 worth) and dumped them into the trash can.

I immediately prepared a cold compress and put it snuggly around my son's neck. I made fomentations out of washcloths for his little chest. I did this several times a day. And in two days Dallas was totally well. This process is part of hydrotherapy, where the hot/cold contrast draws out poisons, while it builds up our immune systems.

God's natural ways are always best. His ways build up our immune systems so they can fight off whatever illness there is.

God made our bodies to be well. He never intended for us to be sick. But in our lifestyle, if we choose something he did **NOT** intend for us to eat, drink, think or do, and we get sick from it, our loving heavenly Father has given us herbs, hydrotherapy, and other natural remedies to help us get well!

> Each one should study carefully the organism of his body, that he may know how to deal intelligently with the body, and that he may be sure that intemperance in eating is not destroying the vital forces of the system. Each one should know for himself how to care properly for the machinery of the body, for no one else can do this for him. (Ellen G. White, *This Day With God*, p. 340)

I am so thankful for God's remedies!

If you are interested in learning more about hydrotherapy, you may find these web tutorials helpful:

"Fomentations," https://1ref.us/rrgl1

"Hydrotherapy Hot Foot Bath," https://1ref.us/244

"The Wonders of Water," https://1ref.us/245

The Illness ♦ 21

God Will Take Care of You

The Influence

This is a story of GOD IN MY LIFE of which I do not yet know the end.

While my husband, son, and I lived in that same apartment as in the previous stories, we always had evening worship. Each evening after supper, Dallas, his daddy, and I sat in the living room and sang the little children's songs that his daddy and I had grown up with, and the ones Dallas was learning each week at our church in his cradle roll class. Then we would read the stories in his children's Sabbath School class lesson paper for that week.

One night, as we were singing and doing the motions to the songs, the doorbell rang. I opened the door, and there stood a young girl that I had never seen before. She said sheepishly, "Hi, I'm Karen, and I live up there above you," and pointed to the apartment above us. "Every night I hear you singing pretty songs with your little boy, and I was wondering if I could join you?"

I welcomed her with open arms and a hug. "Oh, yes, of course you may join us. We would love to have you. Is it OK with your parents?"

She just quietly said, "They aren't home."

Karen came every night. She even started reading the stories to Dallas while I popped popcorn for us to munch on. It turns out that in that upstairs apartment, thirteen-year-old Karen lived with her biological mother and her mother's boyfriend. Both of them worked 3–11 in the evenings. Karen got home from school at 4:00 p.m. to an empty apartment. She was by herself all night, because after her parents got off work, they went out and partied the rest of the night until 4:00 or 5:00 in the morning. Then they came home drunk and went to bed for the morning, until they got up to go back to work in the afternoon.

Karen only saw them briefly in the morning, before she left for school at 7:00 a.m. She was very lonely. She loved having a part in teaching Dallas, and he just loved her too. Karen learned the songs and motions herself while she was teaching Dallas.

One day, God brought to my mind to get a youth magazine for her from church, with stories and puzzles more for her age. Karen loved the stories, so every Sabbath I got a "Little Friend" for Dallas and a "Junior Guide" for Karen. She loved them.

I wanted SO bad to take her to church with us, but her parents were off on Saturdays, and she always stayed home with them in hopes they would include her in their plans for the day. But most of the time, when they finally woke up late in the day, they still went off without her.

One night when Karen came for worship and popcorn, she brought twelve-year-old Mindy. Mindy lived in the building over next to ours, on the first floor also. Mindy had an older brother, Mike, who was fourteen. Mike was very proud of a huge wooden barrel just outside of their apartment's front door on the small patio. The barrel was totally full and running over with empty beer cans that he himself had drunk.

Karen and Mindy came almost every night. They took turns reading to Dallas, then we would have prayer together, holding hands in a circle. After this worship, I would put my little son to bed, then spend the rest of the evening with my two new "daughters." We had so much fun together, talking, laughing, sometimes crying together, and always praying together.

Then one night, Karen was already there singing with Dallas when the doorbell rang. I figured it was Mindy. Opening the door, there stood Mindy with a little girl in her arms. Vassy was three years old. As Mindy was walking to our apartment in the dark, she heard what she thought was a baby crying. She followed the crying sound and found Vassy sitting on her front steps in the dark, because her "parents" had locked her out so they could "have some time together." So, Vassy came with Mindy about every night too. Vassy also loved the stories about Jesus, the songs, and the motions too.

At some point, Karen's half-brother and half-sister came to live with Karen, her mother, and their dad, so they started coming to our evening worship too, which was good, and we enjoyed having them too. But after some time, they moved back to live with their mother, so we did not get to see them again.

One night only Karen came. She did not know where Mindy was. Later that evening, after Dallas was in bed asleep, the doorbell rang. I opened it and there stood "my" twelve-year-old Mindy, dressed like she was twenty-one, high heels, tons of jewelry, fur jacket, super thick makeup. I was just inviting her to come in when she said with tears in her eyes, "I want to thank you for the ONLY home I have EVER had. My folks said I have to make it on my own now, so I don't know anything else to do."

> *Only God knows the full extent of any of our influences on people. It's up to us to make sure our influence on others is a positive one.*

Crying now myself, I begged her to come in and talk about it, to live with us, to let me talk to her parents, or anything! I gave her other options. But her own "parents" told her to go on and be on her own. So, that night, "my" precious Mindy "hit the streets."

Soon after that, my husband took a job back east in Nashville, Tennessee, and we moved away. I received one letter form Karen and wrote her back. But my letter came back, so she had already moved too. It made me sick to lose track of her.

I have always prayed for those precious children—adults now. I had to totally turn them over to God, even though I still cry sometimes when I am praying for them. God knows where they are, and He loves them even more than I do. He can save them if they will let Him. Maybe they will remember (and I pray they do) the little bit they learned of Him at the evening worships and hopefully keep learning His will for them.

Only God knows the full extent of any of our influences on people. It's up to us to make sure our influence on others is a positive one. We can pray every day to God to help us reflect His character in everything we do or say. Thank God that He helps us (if we let Him) to be a good influence on other people.

The Influence ♦ 25

Bring Them In

Alexcenah Thomas, 1885 — William Augustine Ogden

Public Domain
Courtesy of the Cyber Hymnal™

The "Somebody"

We lived in a large neighborhood in Nashville, Tennessee, when my son Dallas was three years old. The bedroom side of our house was only about eight feet from the carport of the next house. There were no screens on our bedroom windows, and we kept our windows open throughout the day for the fresh air and gentle breezes that blew occasionally.

One day, I was working in the kitchen when little Dallas came to me with the startling news, "There's somebody on my pillow."

My heart froze! I did not know the teenage boys next door very well yet and immediately thought the worst. I immediately thought, *I bet one of those boys, or maybe even an adult, has crawled through the unscreened window in Dallas's room and is stealing something!*

Since my husband was at work, I had to be the one to "defend" us, I figured. For lack of anything else, I grabbed the broom, whispered to Dallas, "Be quiet, and stay behind me." Scared and shaking, I tiptoed quietly down the hall with Dallas behind me.

As I got closer to his door, I raised the broom above my head in hopes to bang the intruder on the head as I entered the door and bop him a good one, which would make him drop whatever he was stealing, and run him off. Very tense by now, I whirled around the corner, ready to attack the thief.

To my other surprise—there was no one there!

Dallas came in behind me, still thinking he was supposed to be quiet, and whispered, "See, Mommy, over there," pointing to the pillow on his bed.

There in the middle of his pillow was the "somebody" he was talking about: a praying mantis, looking at us, probably just as frightened as I had been.

Instead of the fight I had anticipated, it turned out to be a great nature study, as my son and I watched and pointed, and talked about all the praying mantis parts and actions. It was so fun to watch!

Then we ushered him back out the window and the "somebody" flew away.

What an exciting ending to our shaky morning.

The Bible talks about eighteen different kinds of insects and their many uses. I'm so glad we got to see one of Gods insects. They are so interesting to study.

This story is a good case of assuming. My daddy taught me not to assume anything, but I didn't think of that at this particular time. I let my imagination build on my false assumption and got my mind thinking entirely wrong, which led to fear. Fear is progressive. But "perfect love casteth out fear" (1 John 4:18). So why assume, imagine, and build fear when we can pray and turn it over to God and know His love will guide us through whatever fear it was that overwhelmed us.

The Stick Horse

My husband, our son Dallas, and I were living in Nashville, Tennessee. It was getting close to Christmastime, and we had no money for our son's third Christmas.

My husband said, "One of my clients owes me $900 for the work I have done for him. He promised to pay me before Christmas."

My husband called him two weeks before Christmas, then one week before Christmas. Still the man said he did not have the money. Finally, three days before Christmas, the man called us and told my husband, "Sorry, I won't be able to give you the money until __after__ Christmas."

Heartbroken, my husband told me the disturbing news. But he said, "Remember, I have that toy metal dump truck with a dump switch and a metal backhoe to go with it that I bought at the truck stop last summer."

(It was an exact replica of the real thing.) So that was good to have for a Christmas present for our little boy.

I started praying that if it was God's will, He would help us to come up with one more gift for our little boy. Immediately, God brought to my mind how much Dallas had begged for a stick horse to ride. He loved horses and had seen one stick horse before in the store.

I loved to sew. I made clothes for my family. Mostly I loved making shirts for my husband and son. I made dress shirts with ties, and western shirts with pretty yolks and matching snaps. I remembered that I had extra material left over from the last western shirt I had made. I got it out, and sure enough there was enough for a horse's head. I sewed it together. Then I realized that I had no stuffing. What could I use to stuff the head? In my dresser drawer, I found scads of nylon stockings and lingerie which, wadded up, made perfect stuffing.

God helped me find some pieces of black felt that I cut to make eyelashes for our horse. I stitched a mouth and nose with black thread. My husband found some very pretty new white cord-size rope for the halter and reins, which slid through the clasps that looked like real halter rings, only smaller. Then I found some black yarn which I sewed on in long, thick loops for a mane. This was all done while Dallas was taking naps. God provided the materials and helped us think of ideas as He helped us find the items around the house.

The horse's head was all finished, but there was no stick to put it on. Dallas was tall for his age, and the stick horse he had tried to ride in the store was two-and-a-half feet and was too short for him. He had the whole stick horse up in the air while he was riding it, instead of the back end of it touching the floor some. It needed to be three feet for him, so he already needed a longer stick than the standard length, that in itself was challenging enough. But nevertheless, there was no stick, long or short.

I toyed in my mind with cutting off the straw end of my broom and using the handle for the stick horse. I probably would have done that, because the broom handle is nice and smooth, so my little boy wouldn't get splinters from it, but that was the only broom we had, and not really wanting to be without a broom for cleaning our floors, I waited. That night, I prayed that God would show me what to do about a smooth stick.

The next morning was Christmas Eve. My husband was going to work till 3:00 p.m. I told him goodbye at the front door. As I watched him drive away, my eyes caught a glimpse of something out in the front yard about fifty feet from our house. It looked for all the world like a straight stick. But any limbs that would fall from the trees in our yard would not be straight, much less smooth, and would break easily. So, I decided that I was "seeing things," and closed the door to go back to breakfast cleanup.

About twenty to thirty minutes later, the thought hit me, *Why don't I just open the front door and look one more time. If the stick is not there, I will know I was "seeing things."* So, I opened the door a little, looked out, and lo and behold, the stick was still there! So, I opened the door all the way, walked out across the yard, and picked up the stick. It was perfectly smooth and straight, just like a broom handle. Only this one was rounded off at **BOTH** ends, not just one.

Barely believing what I was holding in my hands, I took it into the house and measured it. **Guess what?** It was exactly three feet long and perfectly clean. That had to be a stick for a stick horse straight from God!

I stapled the end of the stick into the horse's neck and head with my husband's industrial stapler, wrapped it with Christmas paper, and put it under our artificial Christmas tree. God had supplied another Christmas present for Dallas, and a perfect one at that, with the best stick ever! Dallas could really ride it, and the back of the stick touched the ground like it was supposed to. And it didn't cost us anything!! Dallas loved and rode his stick horse around the house for the next three years, until he totally outgrew it.

Our God even cares about our wants as well as our needs, as long as it is for His honor and glory and for our best good. Don't we serve an awesome God!!!

The Mud

It was springtime in our North Carolina mountains, and we had just had our garden spot plowed up to plant for the season. The next day, the spring showers started, mildly at first, then heavy rains followed, lasting all the rest of that week.

The first day that the sun came out the next week, five-year-old Dallas ran outside to play. Grandpa had bought him a brand-new pair of western boots. So, of course, he wore them all the time, every waking moment that he could. This day was no exception. Dallas put his new cowboy boots on and was out the door to play in the yard. Now and then, he would come in to check on his baby sister, now eight months old. If she was awake, he liked to play with her until she needed to eat or sleep. Then he was out the door again.

I was putting Katy down for her morning nap, when suddenly Dallas started screaming, then broke into heavy crying, somewhere outside the house. With Katy asleep, I ran out the front door and looked to the left side of the house—Dallas was a good fifty feet out into the middle of the garden, sinking down into the mud from the plowed soft dirt that had turned to mud in the torrential rain. Already the mud had swallowed him up to the top of his legs.

How in the world did he get that far out into the garden before he started sinking? I wondered. He must have been running REALLY fast to get that far into the garden. Being spring, and temperatures down in the forties and fifties at night, the mud was really cold and probably freezing his little legs.

> *Finally, I reached Dallas. I tried to pull him out, but with the suction of the mud, I could not budge him!*

I ran out to the garden and tried to step into the mud to go rescue him, but, of course, I started sinking too. I said a quick little prayer for help what to do. Instantly, God brought to my mind that there were some flat boards in the basement. They were only one inch thick and two or three feet long, but perfect for me to carry out several at a time. I ran to the basement and took as many boards as I could carry and placed them one at a time end-to-end on top of the mud to make a path to walk on over the mud to Dallas.

As I walked on them, they started sinking, too, but as I hurried, trying to keep my balance, they quit sinking when I stepped off to the next board. Finally, I reached Dallas. I tried to pull him out, but with the suction of the mud, I could not budge him! I could not pull hard enough to get him out of the mud. I said another little prayer for more strength. I know an angel must have helped me pull my son up out of that mud, because he suddenly came right out with my next pull.

I carried him back to the solid ground of the yard. Through his tears, he was screaming, "My boots, Mommy, my boots, get my boots!" The mud had kept his boots! So, back I went across the (now partly buried) boards, barefoot so I would not lose my shoes, too, as the boards were sinking in that very cold mud. At the end of the last board, I looked down to see only mud! The mud had caved in on top of wherever the boots were. I got down very carefully on my knees on that one board. That was slowly sinking, too, as I tried to balance my weight on one six-inch-wide board. I thrust my hand and arm into the mud to feel for the boots. Down, down I dug until the mud was above my elbow line, praying all the time that God would help me find my son's boots. Suddenly, I felt something that was NOT mud!

I got a hold of it and pulled and pulled. Out came the first boot, FULL OF MUD! And then I thrust my hand into the mud again, and just like He always does, God put my hand right on the second boot! And I pulled it out too!

By now, the board that I was on had sunk into the mud, and my legs and feet were in the cold mud. But thankfully, God worked it all out and got me and both boots back to solid ground!

After a lot of cleanup, Dallas and I were clean, dry, and warm, and "none the worse for the wear."

Dallas and I learned a valuable lesson that day. Just because the ground "looks" solid, does not always mean it is. Check it out first.

It is the same with life—just because something "seems" OK to do, does not always mean it is! Check with God first before venturing out into something new.

HE NEVER LEADS US ASTRAY.

The Sled

It was wintertime in the mountains of North Carolina, and we had one of our biggest and best winters. The snow was two feet deep and had frozen over throughout the night. The next morning, after breakfast, Baby Katy had gone to sleep for her morning nap. I thought that this would be a good time to take five-year-old Dallas sledding on our beautiful snow. So, we got all bundled up and put our winter boots and mittens on. Thankfully, we always prayed to God every morning to protect us and guard our day.

    Outside, my son and I got out our wooden sled from the garage. Our backyard is sloped down from the house to the woods and makes a good short run for sledding, which Dallas and I had enjoyed several times together. But today, I thought it would be fun to do one of the two longer snowy trails that go down the hill in the woods behind our house.

I said, "Dallas, let's do this trail over here," pointing to the first woodsy trail.

"Oh, goody, Mommy!" He had never done that one before but had wanted to.

This particular trail starts at the edge of our backyard, goes about ten feet down to the side, then curves to the right, and goes straight down a steeper slope another 100 feet or so to the five-foot-wide creek. The trail goes over the creek on a two-foot-wide wooden bridge. The creek this time of year was about three feet deep and frozen over. I sat down on the sled at the back and put Dallas in front of me—to help him stay on it and keep him safe. I held the rope to steer and put my legs around little Dallas to hold him in, with my feet on the wooden steering column on the front of the sled to be able to turn the sled at the curve.

I pushed us off, and away we went! Dallas was so excited, laughing and squealing, "Wheeeee!"

We made the curve just fine and picked up speed as we sailed down the hill. Just as we approached the bridge over the creek, the sled hit a tree root (that I didn't see in time to miss) protruding up out of the snow, which shot the sled off the trail and plunged it and us straight into the creek, breaking through the ice.

Being on the front, Dallas was thrown forward and totally submerged into the icy water! He came up screaming with fright and gasping for air. I pulled him out of the water and ran back up the hill, carrying my frozen and teeth-chattering little boy. In the house I took his wet clothes off and wrapped him in blankets. I sat close to the cozy, warm wood stove and held my still chattering little son—singing and talking to him and telling stories until his freezing and fright were gone.

I have always heard, "When you fall off a horse, get right back on until you conquer the fear of the situation." So, now, since Katy was still napping peacefully, my son and I bundled up again, and headed out to sled the second snowy trail.

Reluctantly, Dallas sat back down on the sled. I wrapped my legs around him once again and prepared to steer. This trail, though just as steep as the other one, is different. It doesn't cross the creek, it just winds in and out around the trees. I pushed off again and away we went. Dallas, all excited again, was laughing happily.

At first, I was doing OK dodging the trees. But as we picked up speed, my foot pressure on the steering column was not strong enough to miss one tree. We hit the tree full force, throwing little Dallas, face first straight into the tree. Whimpering, but trying *so very hard* not to cry, my brave son looked at me as he said shakily, "Mommy, do you care if I don't ride on the front anymore?"

Bless his little heart! It's a wonder he ever went sledding again, but he did. As he grew up, he dearly loved sledding. He and his friends would go all the way to the top of our mountain and sled down the road before the state ever started grading it.

We were so thankful to God that He kept Dallas from hypothermia, being totally submerged in that icy water, and thankful that, even though bruised and hurting, God kept his little face bones from being shattered and no broken nose from the tree. We were so thankful to God that He protected all our family through all those sledding years.

We sure serve a loving and awesome God!!

The Cake

Both my children loved homemade ice cream cakes. So, it was no surprise that Dallas asked if I would make an ice cream cake for this upcoming eighth birthday.

Now, the ice cream cakes that I made back then were in the form of a tube cake, except it is about eight inches tall, and about six inches across the top, pyramiding down to seven or eight inches across the bottom. So, one ice cream cake fed eight people with hearty slices, ten people maximum with smaller slices.

So, in figuring this, I told Dallas, "OK, honey, you can invite six of your little friends to your birthday party," thinking that would work out fine to have six friends plus his little sister, Katy and himself for the eight pieces of cake. Dallas named six of his friends, and we invited them. All six of them accepted and said they would come.

The party day came. Everyone in our house was excited. The supper was all cooked, the ice cream cake was all made and in the freezer, and all of us were laughing and jabbering away as we put up and arranged the last of the party decorations. By afternoon, everything was ready.

The first little guest arrived and knocked on the door. As I opened it, the little girl came bounding in all excited. Her mother, who was dropping her off at the door, said, "OK if I stay too?"

Totally shocked, and not having thought of anyone extra coming to the party, I couldn't tell any mother "No, you can't stay with your child," so, I smiled and said, "Oh yes, please do," as I opened the door wider. Happily, she came in.

The next child came bounding in as I opened the door. His mother AND his dad had "walked" him to the door. "We always love to come here; he has so much fun! Mind if we just stay too?"

"Oh, yes, of course."

To my utter shock and dismay, all six children arrived on time, bringing with them parents, siblings, and one mother also brought five other children she was babysitting that day. More and more children and adults poured into our living room until there were twenty-six people at Dallas's party for six.

Wonder why I EVER thought that one ice cream cake would be enough!

Of course, having all those people made a whole lot more fun for all the games we played outside. After the games, we all went back into the house for supper. Thankfully I had fixed tons of food, so there was plenty for everyone.

But then, it came time for the cake. Everyone was laughing and talking together as I went into the kitchen. No one had any idea there would not be enough cake/ice cream.

I had been praying silently to God through the whole party saying, "God, do something, PLEASE, do something. I am so sorry that I did not think about more people coming. PLEASE do something. It would not be right for me to give ice cream cake to some guests and not to the others. PLEASE, GOD, DO SOMETHING!"

I took the cake out of the freezer, put the candles on top, and lit them. After we sang happy birthday to Dallas, he blew out the candles. I carried the ice cream cake back into the kitchen to cut it. By now, I was almost in tears that I had not made at least two or three cakes and was going to have to hurt someone's feelings.

My friend, Ginger, followed me into the kitchen. She said, "Did you make two?"

I said, "No."

She said, "What are you going to do?"

I said, "I don't know but," smiling now, "God is going to do something."

Right then, Jan, another mother, came into the kitchen to help.

I started slicing the ice cream cake. I laid the first slice on the paper plate; Ginger put a fork/spoon on it, handed it to Jan, who picked up a napkin from the stack and took it all out to the first person in the living room. I sliced the next piece of cake, and the next piece, laying them each on a plate and each one was taken out to guests. Still praying silently, I continued to slice. No one else in the party had any idea what was happening in the kitchen. Back in the living room, the guests were all having a great time talking and laughing as the party continued.

One by one, two by two, the plates went out to the people. Both helpers asked periodically, "Do you think there is going to be enough?"

One by one, two by two, the plates went out to the people. Both helpers asked periodically, "Do you think there is going to be enough?"

I always answered, "I don't know."

I kept slicing and praying silently. After ten pieces had gone out in the living room, it looked like that much was STILL THERE on the cake plate. Each time I sliced and put another piece of ice cream cake on a plate, it looked like it was still there on the cake plate. The cake just kept being there!

At one point, when Jan came back into the kitchen, I asked her, "How many more do we need?"

She counted from the kitchen door and said, "Twelve." Sometime later, after I laid the last piece of cake on its plate, I anxiously asked, "Wonder how many more we need?"

Just then, Jan came back into the kitchen, took the plate, and said, "This is all we need." God had made that eight- to ten-slice cake serve twenty-six people!! We sure serve an awesome God!!

This birthday cake story is a small-scale repeat of our God's miracles in the Bible; like the stories of Jesus feeding all of the 5,000 people with the little boy's lunch of five barley loaves and two small fishes (Matt. 14:15–21; Luke 9:10–17; John 6:5–14).

Also, the miracle that happened to the widow of Zarephath, when she was preparing the last oil in the cruse and the last flour in the barrel to make a cake of bread for her and her son to eat, and then they expected to die because they had no more food. But because she obeyed God and unselfishly gave that last cake of bread to Elijah, God replaced the oil in the cruse and the flour in the barrel. And there was enough each day for the three of them: Elijah, the widow, and her son for the rest of the famine (1 Kings 17:8–16).

Yes, friend, God is in your life and in my life working miracles, just like He did in the Bible. Watch for them.

The Arm

Sometimes, when driving a semitruck across country, my husband, the children's daddy, would not get back home for five or six weeks. He would drive back and forth across the United States, east to west, and west to east, carrying various commercial loads, never coming close enough to our home in North Carolina to come by to see us.

On one of these occasions, after being gone for six weeks already, our daddy was coming home. Our young children were so very excited. The day before he was to arrive, they cleaned their rooms especially well. They made little "Welcome Home" signs, "I Love You, Daddy" posters, and "We Missed You, Daddy" pictures, placing them strategically all over the house.

The night before he was to come, Dallas, Katy, and I were so ecstatic; we could barely quiet down enough to go to sleep. But finally, the house was totally quiet as we all drifted off into a deep sleep.

A few hours later, I was suddenly awakened by the ringing of the telephone. As I picked up the receiver, I glanced at the clock. It was 2 o'clock in the morning.

"Hello," I said groggily.

On the other end of the phone, my husband was saying something, but what was it? In my excitement of hearing his voice, I wasn't comprehending at first what he was saying.

"I am in Georgia, just unloaded in Atlanta." (Just three hours away from us.) I was so excited! But then he said, "I was just getting ready to drive home, but dispatch just told me that they had a load for me to take to California, so I'm gonna take it. I won't be coming home tonight."

My heart sank! Continuing on, he said, "I have to hurry, don't have time to talk now. I love you, bye." And hung up.

For a moment, I just sat there, Indian style, in the middle of the bed, in a total fog, just staring into space. What just happened? My mind was trying to wake up and comprehend it all. As that devastating news began to sink in, I started to cry. Such a letdown, such a disappointment! The children would be SO disappointed, so heartbroken in the morning when they woke up. They had gone to bed that night singing their made-up song, "Daddy's coming home! Daddy's coming home!"

As I started coming around to reality, I realized I was cold—the house was cold. Obviously, the fire in the woodstove had gone out. It was our only heat, and it was 20° outside, but I didn't even care! At that moment, I didn't care if I lived or died. As I sat there crying, I thought to myself, *I'll just sit here and freeze to death. It doesn't even matter. No one will even care.* My crying was uncontrollable by now, and I just wanted to die, I thought. In my selfish desperation, I cried out to God, "God, please send someone to hold me."

Instantly, a big huge arm slid slowly around me, covering my whole back and sides and embraced me. Immediately, I was snug and warm as toast and so very incredibly secure. A wonderful, indescribable peace came over me!

> *I never saw the arm there in the darkness, but I FELT it!*

"And the peace of God, which passeth all understanding, shall keep your hearts and minds through Christ Jesus" (Phil. 4:7).

My crying stopped, my happiness returned, I definitely wanted to live. Immediately, I started planning fun things that I and the children could do that next day, after we got up, to make up for their disappointment too.

Obviously, I had not thought through my request to God to send someone to hold me. What if a stranger had showed up at my front door at such an early hour? It would have really been unnerving.

I never saw the arm there in the darkness, but I FELT it! I have no idea how long that big, heavenly arm was around me, but it was perfect, and timed exactly right—as is everything God does.

With God's help, my hope and courage returned. I jumped out of bed and started a fire in the woodstove, and pretty soon the house was getting warm. I went back to bed and slept, peaceful and content, for the rest of the night.

WOW! Just think how much God cares! He loves each one of us the same—you and me. Remember, dear friend, God DOES truly love YOU! And He is definitely in your life too—when you're happy, when you're sad, when you're anxious, when you're discouraged—He is there in ALL your situations.

God says that He loves us so much that He is trying to draw us back to Himself with His outstretched arm. "I will redeem you with a STRETCHED OUT ARM" (Exod. 6:6, emphasis mine. Also see

Deuteronomy 7:19). He wants to be our God and He wants us to be His people. Maybe that's the arm I felt. It is so warm, comforting, peaceful, and loving. It's EVERYTHING we need.

Talk to Him every day, all day long. Remember, the more you talk to someone, the closer you get to each other. The same with God: the more you talk to Him, the closer you get to Him. God loves you dearly, and wants to spend time with you, so LET HIM!

"Thou wilt keep him in perfect peace, whose mind is stayed on thee: because he trusteth in thee" (Isa. 26:3).

The Move

One day, when the children were gone to school, I was down the slight slope behind the house, hanging up the freshly washed clothes on the clothesline, when something caught my eye. I turned around and looked back toward the house, and there was a big, black line across the green grass, about halfway between me and the house. AND it was moving ACROSS the yard. It was too even, too straight, and too wide to be a snake. The line was about five inches wide and approximately three feet long. It was solid black with little white dots throughout the middle part of the black line.

I put the clothes and the clothespins in my hand back down into the clothes basket, and walked slowly, and cautiously toward the moving black line. As I got closer, to my shock and delight, it was a whole colony of black ants, obviously moving their whole colony across the yard to a new "neighborhood" hole.

Of course, I don't know for sure, but humanly thinking, it could have been the group of men first, maybe the leaders and fathers of the colony, leading the procession at the first third of the procession. Then the middle third of the group was the nurses carrying the tiny white newborns. Then followed lastly by the women, I guess, mothers, and teachers, all moving in unison in one thick line.

WOW! What a miracle to watch! They marched all the way across the backyard and went down, a few at a time, into another hole in the ground on the other side of the yard.

Thinking back, I'm still amazed at how organized and cooperative those ants were with each other! Not that I would have understood the language anyway—but I didn't hear one complaining word! Even by the way they were cooperating and staying in line, walking together in unison, and no out of place movement like someone causing a ruckus, showing no one was complaining, "I'm tired" or "do I have to do this?"

WOW! Wouldn't it be great if we as humans got along that well together?

Solomon in the Bible, the wisest man that ever lived, said, "Go to the ant, thou sluggard; consider [observe] her ways, and be wise: Which, having no guide [chief], overseer [officer], or ruler, provideth [prepares] her meat [food] in the summer, and gathereth her food in the harvest" (Prov. 6:6–8). This is an example for us of diligence and perseverance.

ଔଔଔ ❖ ଓଓଓ

Another day, my cousin Joyce and I were walking in the early morning up our little side road called Autumn View Court, when Joyce discovered a small black line crossing that road. This line was only about two and a half to three inches long. It was many tiny little worms, each about the length of the nail on your smallest toe (about one-fourth of an inch, maybe), all crawling constantly together, over, under, and around each other, all the while moving forward in unison. One line of worms, maybe 100 of them, moving forward, all the time slithering all over each other at the same time, still getting wherever they were going.

WOW! What an organized God we serve! He made all nature to be at peace and organized!

Doing My Best

Vs. 1 George Cooper; Vss. 2-11 Jennifer Dietrich

J. R. Sweney

1. I am just a tiny cricket, Chirping in a shady thicket, There I take my rest.
2. I am just a little flower, Blooming during sun or shower, Quietly I'm dressed.

Many songs are clearer, prouder, Many voices sweeter, louder, But I do my best.
Many flowers grow much taller, Many bloom in colors brighter, But I do my best.

Refrain
Doing my best, doing my best, Jesus always helps me do my best;
In the path of doing duty There is so much joy and beauty; So I do my best!

3. I am just a salmon silver,
   Swimming up a rushing river,
   It's so cold and wet.
   Oh, these rapids are such trouble,
   But my efforts I'll redouble,
   I won't give up yet.

4. I am just a little turtle,
   Dwelling in a forest fertile,
   Creeping as I go.
   I must never stop to grumble,
   Though my life is very humble,
   And I'm very slow.

5. I am just a small brown acorn,
   Buried in the dirt, forlorn,
   Where no one can see.
   I won't mourn that I am hidden,
   I will grow as God has bidden,
   I will be a tree.

6. I am just a little earthworm,
   Out of sight I'm quick to squirm,
   Hiding from the light.
   I will never cease my toil,
   Making better dirt and soil,
   Using all my might.

7. I am just a playful kitty,
   And my coat is very pretty,
   Made of softest fur.
   Other animals are stronger,
   And there's some that live much longer,
   But they cannot purr.

8. I am just a beetle bashful,
   But I can do something helpful,
   While I'm passing by.
   Other lights are bigger, brighter,
   But are any really nicer
   Than a firefly?

9. I am just a little fellow,
   Basking in a sunny meadow,
   Lizard is my name.
   Eating bugs is all my labor,
   That's how I can help my neighbor,
   Every day the same.

10. I am just a toad in springtime,
    Hiding in the muck and slime,
    That's my place to rest.
    Life for me is not so thrilling,
    But I will not stop my trilling,
    Till I've done my best.

11. I am just a simple lichen,
    But I teach a helpful lesson,
    Though I cannot talk.
    Raging storms may fell an oak tree,
    But they cannot ever hurt me,
    Clinging to the rock.

The Friend

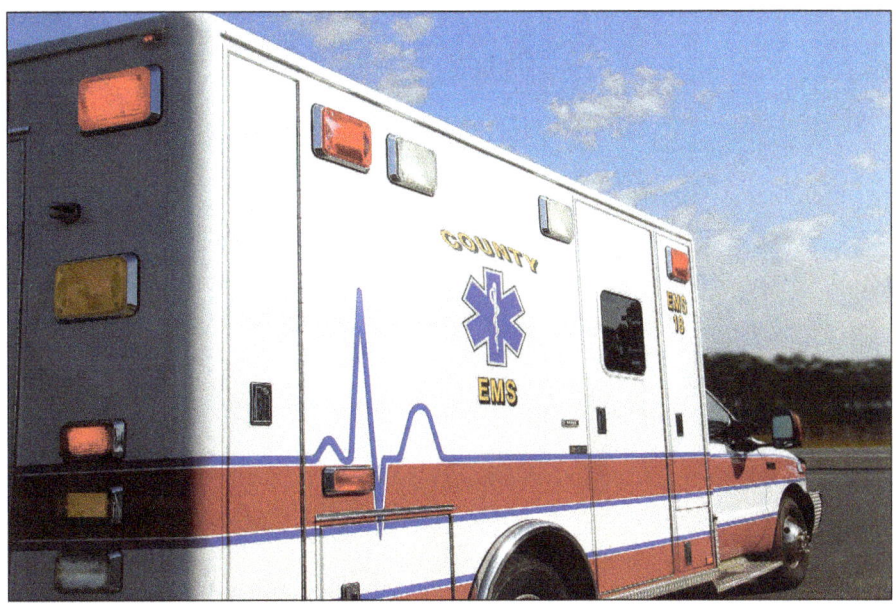

A good friend, Dr. Bill Moore, came with some other friends into the lobby of Fletcher Park Inn where I was standing in the buffet line. He said excitedly to me, "Have we got an exciting miracle story for you!" And here is the story he told me:

> *It was a beautiful Sabbath day in our North Carolina mountains in the middle of August. My wife, Janis, and I took her mother, Dorothy, to Crossville, Tennessee, to visit some long-lost relatives, Brian and Ruthie, as well as Brian's mom whom Dorothy had not seen in forty years. We had a great day catching up and reviving so many memories.*
>
> *About 5:00 p.m., as we were leaving, we were descending the outside steps at Brian and Ruthie's house. We were going down single file with Ruthie leading, followed by Janis, Dorothy, Brian, and lastly me.*

About five steps from the bottom, Dorothy suddenly lost her balance or something. She turned and flew through the air, landing flat on her back on the concrete below. Then her head hit, sounding like a melon hitting the concrete. Immediately, Janis was on her right side, Brian at her head, and I was on her left side monitoring her radial pulse. Janis was calling to her mom, but Dorothy was unconscious, and not breathing. She was turning blue and had a very fast, thready pulse. Janis was just about to start rescue breathing when Dorothy gurgled and blood gushed from her mouth and nose. There was no way to give her a breath. Her pulse got slower and slower ... and then stopped.

> **There was no way to give her a breath. Her pulse got slower and slower ... and then stopped.**

I said, "She's gone!" Instantly, Brian (who was a nondenominational minister of a small church there in Crossville), placed both hands on Dorothy's head and cried out to the Lord. I don't recall what he said, but immediately Dorothy's pulse came back strong and steady. There was no more bleeding. In fact, the blood seemed to have disappeared. Dorothy started breathing and "pinked up."

Ruthie had been on the phone with 911 this whole time, and an ambulance was on its way. Dorothy was taken by helicopter to the medical center in Knoxville, Tennessee, where she remained unconscious for three days, until Tuesday morning. She suddenly woke up and asked where she was and what was going on. After a few days later, she was transported to Asheville, North Carolina (closer to her home), where she received six weeks of rehab at a rehab center, after which she came home to her basement apartment in our home and resumed her daily routine.

She still lives with us and is a daily reminder that there is a God in heaven who loves each one of us. He always hears our prayers and performs unmistakable miracles!

About six months after Dorothy's fall, death, miraculous return to life, and rehab, she fell in her kitchen onto the ceramic tile floor, breaking her elbow. It wasn't a severe injury and only required a sling to be worn about a month. Then six months after that, she fell again, breaking her wrist. Once again, she only needed to wear a removable cast for a few weeks. A few months later, she broke her right hip. Fortunately, she wasn't in a great deal of pain. We called 911 for the ambulance to come transport *her to the hospital, where she had a quick 20-minute surgery to have pins placed in her broken femur.*

With all these unfortunate events, I began to ponder why God would bring her back to life. I wasn't doubting God's judgment, for I know He loves us very much, and only has our best interest at heart. As usual, God had a way of answering my prayers and thoughts.

Kathy Lynch, one of the ladies who helped care for Dorothy during the week related the following story to me:

One morning, she arrived at Dorothy's apartment to find a pile of wet bed clothes and towel and washcloth on the floor in the corner of the bathroom. Kathy then woke Dorothy up to start her day and asked Dorothy about it.

Dorothy said she had gotten up in the night to go to the bathroom, fell on the bathroom floor, and could not get up. She called and called for Janis to come downstairs to help her, but Janis could not hear her and did not come, so she urinated on herself and the floor. Then "someone" showed up and helped her get up, washed her off, dressed her in a clean, dry gown, and tucked her back into bed. The clean gowns were in the dresser drawer in the bedroom. Then the person cleaned the floor and put all the wet things into the corner of the bathroom in an unusual circular shaped pile.

Dorothy said the person who helped her was extremely patient, kind, and gentle with her. Dorothy repeatedly kept asking Kathy if Janis had come downstairs. Kathy came upstairs to talk with Janis about it and found out it wasn't Janis at all who helped Dorothy. There was no one there to help except her guardian angel.

After all of this, I said, "OK, Lord, I'll quit questioning Your judgment. You have Dorothy in the palm of Your hand. She's yours!"

Don't we serve an AWESOME GOD?! Now, after hearing Dr. Bill Moore's story, we all want to be sure to find out who is this modern "good Samaritan." Maybe an angel; maybe Dorothy's own angel; maybe Jesus Himself. We will find out when we all get to heaven.

The Dresses

When my daughter, Katy, was in her early teens, I took her to a large chain department store to buy a Sabbath dress for her. She had grown out of her other Sabbath dresses. This particular store was having a fantastic seasonal sale of 75 percent off. We found some dresses her size that she really liked and bought them. And then, since they were marked down so much, we went ahead and checked out my size. Lo and behold! We found first one dress marked down from $92 to $10! Then another pretty one marked the same price! Then, one more really pretty one marked down from $94 to $12. So, even I got three new dressy church dresses that would have been $278 for the three—and was charged only $32. WOW! We were both so excited for these wonderful deals!

I wore those three dresses (alternately, of course) for a few years. They never, ever wore out. I was so thankful for them. Through the years, different people would compliment me on them from time to time. All three dresses were modest and very feminine and pretty. *Just perfect for me*, I thought.

Then one day, some time after their purchase, God told me to give those three dresses away. GIVE THEM AWAY! But I LOVE those dresses! Then He told me to give them to my friend Linda.

GIVE THEM TO MY FRIEND! WHY? Why could SHE have them and I could not? Why were they suddenly better for her and not for me? Selfishly, I argued MY feelings.

God answered, "Because you meet different people than she does."

"So what? What difference does that make? Of course we meet different people."

Patiently, quietly, God said, "These dresses will be a stumbling block to someone you meet." Oh my! I never thought of that before. Of course, I do not want to be a stumbling block to anyone.

I reasoned to myself, *They were such a good deal, and, after all, I am still getting compliments on each one as I wear it*. I did not hesitate to talk about the good deal when people gave me compliments. Not one time did I ever give God the credit for the "good deals" nor for showing the dresses to me in the first place. Not realizing it, I had basically made an idol of them, as you can see by my arguing with God. Those three dresses meant more to me than my very own God and Savior did!

Even though those three dresses served a good purpose, and were perfect for me in my eyes, was I willing to give them up for HIM? Or would I think more of my dresses than I did of my Maker and God? Even though at first, I did not understand, and I thought God's request was unfair, I realize now that all of that was for HIS honor and glory, and for MY best good, to teach me to be more humble, and hopefully, I was not a stumbling block to anyone.

My friend, Linda, was a single mother trying to raise her teenage son alone. I took the three dresses on hangers over to her house. She was thrilled to get them.

She said, "Oh my! These are so pretty! Don't you want them?"

Of course, I wanted them, I thought. But I just said, "I want you to have them, if you want them."

She said, "Oh, yes, I do!" And just beamed! She tried them on and was so excited that they fit perfectly and looked very nice on her! Seeing her so happy made me happy to be sharing them with her.

Later, God did provide another pretty and more conservative dress for me to wear to church. He showed it to me, in a secondhand store, and it was on the markdown rack, "Fifty cents just for today!" That dress also lasted for many years.

Looking back, I can see how God was testing me to see if I "have no other gods before him": His first law (Exod. 20:3).

I almost let myself become like Satan and his angels because I had self-will and pride.

"Self-will and pride are evils that turned angels into demons and barred the gates of heaven against them" (*Sons and Daughters of God*, p. 115).

His promise is "Blessed are the poor in spirit [humble]: for theirs is the kingdom of heaven" (Matt. 5:3).

Thank You, God in heaven, for not giving up on me! Please keep teaching me Your way.

Long Ago in Old Judea

UNISON SONG

Mrs. J. M. Bittle
J. H. Fillmore

1. Long ago in old Judea, By the shores of Galilee, Jesus spake unto the fishers: "Leave your nets and follow Me." Still there comes the blessed story, Pealing thro' the ages dim: Who of you will leave your pleasures, Take your cross and follow Him?

2. Now no more in old Judea Jesus walketh by the sea; But He calleth, ever calleth: "Who will come and follow Me?" Come to Jesus—time may tarnish Many a dream of beauty fair; What He offers fadeth never— Life eternal over there.

3. Over there, beyond death's billows, Eyes of faith can plainly see The bright mansions where He promised All His followers should be. Let us heed the gospel story, Pealing thro' the ages dim: "Jesus loves you! died to save you! Give up all and follow Him."

The Dream

Through the years, I thought that I was doing what I was supposed to do, what God wanted me to do. Then God gave me a dream to show me how I was actually doing—the REAL me.

In this dream, it was as if I was watching a video. I was watching from behind Jesus, over His shoulder. I was seeing myself walking slowly towards Him. Jesus had His right arm outstretched, with His right hand on my left side, guiding me toward Him.

Suddenly, I stopped walking and went into a frenzy, my arms waving in all directions as I loudly expressed my worry: "Oh no!" I yelled. "What am I going to do about this problem?" I ranted and raved, floundering around like a fish out of water and stopped walking. Then Jesus quietly removed His hand from my side and pulled His arm back to Himself, holding it across His waist, waiting patiently.

After a while, I finally quieted down; then Jesus extended His arm, touching my side, guiding me again, and all was peaceful and quiet.

Then suddenly, I thought of a dilemma, and I stopped walking toward Him again and yelled out, "Oh dear! What's going to happen about THAT situation?" And again, I was all in a dither, with my arms waving in all directions, and I went all to pieces in my worry.

Again Jesus removed His guiding hand and took it back to Himself.

Finally, I calmed down. Once again, very calmly, Jesus stretched His arm out and gently placing His hand to my side, started guiding me toward Him.

This happened three different times in the dream. Each time, my frenzy was for a different reason—reasons that were very real to me at the time. After I calmed down the third time, I woke up.

As soon as I woke up, the first thought that God put into my mind was *WHY don't I let Jesus lead me ALL THE TIME?* Everything was so calm, so loving, so organized, so stress-free while Jesus was leading me! My patient, tender Savior; my gentle, loving King Jesus LOVES ME. He wants me to love Him enough to obey Him and let Him guide me totally and constantly through this rough world's anxieties, sufferings, disappointments, and all of the problems going on in my life now and forever. When the worries, anxieties, and problems hit, all I have to do is look to Him and keep looking to Him, dwell on His love for me, His gentleness, His patience, His kindness toward me. Then I, too, will be more loving, more gentle, more patient, and more kind. "[By] beholding, we become changed" (*Christ's Object Lessons*, p. 355). See 2 Corinthians 3:18.

If we behold (dwell on) impatience, roughness, hatred, anger, anxiety, then we, too, become that way. But if we behold (dwell on) Christ's love for us, His kindness, His patience, then we too will become like Him.

I thought, *Hey then, why don't I start praying for those personality traits, those life-changing things that the Bible calls "fruit of the spirit," 'But the fruit of the Spirit is love, joy, peace, longsuffering, gentleness, goodness, faith, meekness, temperance: against such there is no law' (Gal. 5:22–23). If I pray for them, God will give them to me.* Why don't YOU pray for them too? And watch Him work in your life too? It's worth a try.

The different reasons for my worry—that was so real to me when they were happening—were still real but less and less stressful as I let HIM handle them. In fact, looking back now, they were handled so calmly by my Maker, they were almost nonexistent. I am the one that was making the huge mountains out of mole hills, because I was not letting God lead me all those times.

1 Peter 5:7 says, "Casting all your care upon him; for he careth for you." Then the next verse says, "Be sober, be vigilant; because your adversary the devil, as a roaring lion, walketh about, seeking whom he may devour." God loves and cares for me and will handle ALL my cares, worries, and situations, if I just turn them over to Him and let Him.

So, see, dear friend, if we do not give all our cares and worries to God and let Him handle them, then Satan, who is our adversary—our enemy—will come in and mess with our mind, getting us into that frenzied worry, helping us to develop headaches and ulcers of the stomach and worse. So, it even affects our health.

Remember, dear "stressed-out" friend, God not only loves you dearly, He will also take care of ALL the stresses in your life. Just turn them over to Him and let Him.

While you have your Bible open, read on in verses 9, 10, and 11 of 1 Peter 5. It's so encouraging.

Remember, dear "stressed-out" friend, God not only loves you dearly, He will also take care of ALL the stresses in your life. Just turn them over to Him and let Him.

The Dent

One summer day, right after Katy had graduated from her senior year at Fletcher Academy, she had driven into Hendersonville, our local city, to do some shopping. I had also gone to the same city to run some errands.

I called her on my cell phone to ask a question. It turned out that we both were in the same area, so we decided to meet each other in a certain parking lot on Four Seasons Boulevard. I arrived there first, so I pulled my Buick Le Sabre up and parked at the far end of a row of other parked cars and turned my car motor off to wait for Katy to come.

Shortly, she came from the other direction in her Jeep Wrangler. She pulled right up at an angle beside me facing the opposite direction, not totally parallel with me, where both of our driver doors were facing across from each other. Since my motor was off, I opened my door far enough to be able to talk, and Katy rolled her window down so we could hear each other. After our conversation was over, she started backing up slowly, so as not to brush the back of my car with the front of hers, as she drove off. Not being totally parallel with my car, her Jeep's front end was angled slightly toward the back end of my car, so Katy backed up some to pull away from my car. Neither of us saw that my open driver door was against her Jeep, as she backed up, the edge of my door caught the grooved handle of her door, and her backing up was pushing my half-opened car door into the fender of my car, making a deeper and deeper dent as she backed up. Katy was watching in her rearview mirror, so did not see what was happening there at the side.

When I saw it, I screamed, "Katy! Stop!" She slammed on the brakes, and then turned to see what was happening. The dent in my fender was about six inches long and about three inches deep already by then and would have become deeper and deeper if she had kept backing up farther. Thankfully, God helped us to see it in time to stop before it got any worse.

My heart sank as I realized my car was ruined and would cost lots of money (that I did not have) to fix. Also, I realized right then that until I could get it fixed, the door would not even close, crammed into the fender that way.

Katy quickly put her Jeep back into first gear and started pulling forward slowly so, hopefully, not to do more damage. As she pulled forward, releasing my car door from her Jeep—to our utter amazement—my car door also pulled out of the dent (which was a miracle in itself). Right before our very eyes, the dent came out too! My car door came right out into place, releasing the dent, which also, at the same time, smoothed right out as the door edge came right out of it! I was literally watching a miracle happening with my very own eyes!

When the Jeep was totally pulled away and separated from my car door, then my car door was totally straight and worked just fine! We both jumped out of our cars to look at the deep dent in my car's fender, and it was not there! There was no dent, and no scratch at all! It was perfectly smooth!

WOW! What a demonstration of God's power and love for us (His rushed, paying-no-attention people). "[B]efore they call, I will answer; and while they are yet speaking, I will hear" (Isa. 65:24).

The Rooms

My husband and my son had been building onto our house when my husband left. He had just started to make a kitchen out of one of the new rooms that they had built on.

I love to design rooms and houses, but I have no idea how to build them. So, the two rooms intended for the kitchen and dining room sat empty and unfinished for a couple of years, not even paint on the walls. There were not cabinets nor anything in the "hoped-to-be kitchen." We did, however, have our table and chairs in the unfinished dining room.

My daughter, Katy, worked for our dentist, Dr. Bill Moore. He arranged for his employees to go to Charleston, South Carolina, for a week's conference. Their seminars were over on Friday, so Katy and Mary, her coworker, stayed in the hotel room that they had for the conference week, and our friend, Anna, and I drove down on Friday and shared their room for the weekend.

We had so much fun—all four of us together. In the evenings we toured the streets of the old part of town, admiring the beautiful houses built in the mid-eighteenth century.

One thing I noticed was that most of the houses had at least one or more rooms with striped wallpaper on the walls. It looked sooo pretty to me! I loved it!

So, when we got back home, Katy and I talked about those unfinished rooms in our house, which now had become storage with boxes in them. We talked about making a quaint little parlor out of the kitchen room because we actually needed more visiting/sitting area, since the living room wasn't quite big enough anymore, and we could still use our small kitchen already there in the original house.

We prayed about it to ask God's opinion and approval. We wanted to be good stewards for Him with the money He always provided for us at the right time. We didn't want to be frivolous and waste any money. God opened the doors as we proceeded with our plans. Count His many blessings in just this one story!

I didn't know anything about wallpaper, so the day I was to go look for wallpaper, I prayed that God would guide me to the right store and help me to know what wallpaper to choose. He brought to mind a place that sold wallpaper. So, I drove over there. But before I walked in, I prayed that God would have me see first thing what He wanted me to buy (so I wouldn't have a chance to get mixed up on several selections and get confused).

I walked into the store, up to the counter, and asked the lady about seeing some wallpaper. She reached down into a box right where she was standing behind the counter and held up a roll of the prettiest wallpaper I had ever seen! I had an idea already in my mind from the walls I had seen in the older houses. But this one was totally different than what I had pictured, and so very pretty!

The clerk said, "Someone just had this out, looking at it, and I had not put it back on the shelf yet."

It was a pretty royal green stripe with thin gold edging on each side of the inch-wide green stripe and a tint of gold sparkle in the gold edging. Plus, it was on sale! I said, "Yes! That's it! That's what I want!"

I asked about a border. Then she held up a roll of border to go with the wallpaper. It was perfect, too! It had different shades of pink and mauve flowers on a background of that same royal green color, with tints of gold sparkle. Just perfect! And it was on sale too!

Instead of spending precious hours looking and deciding, God had me in and out of that store in twenty minutes with the beautiful purchase, and the cost was almost half the cost of what I had planned to spend! Isn't our God wonderful?!

But that's not all! Remember, we prayed for God's guidance in fixing up these new rooms? The very next day, when our painter friend, John, came up to see about helping with the room—he looked at the wallpaper and said, "I just finished painting a room for one of my customers that exact same green! I have a bucket full left over that you can just have! And I'll paint it for you for NOTHING." (See God working?) So, a day was decided on to start on the room.

John painted the lower three feet of the walls that pretty green. Then we left it to dry for a couple of days.

The ceiling of that room had a couple of long holes where the ceiling boards did not meet. John had a good idea. He covered the holes by covering the entire ceiling in a pretty pattern with 1 x 6 inch boards and painting just those boards the same green as the bottom part of the wall. So, it made a pretty green lattice pattern on the white ceiling, kind of like one of the ceilings in "America's Castle" that we all love, about twenty miles from our house. (God did it again!)

Katy and I knew nothing about hanging wallpaper, but God interceded again. A friend, Kristy, who had not called in ages, called to say hi one day. While we were talking, I mentioned about the wallpaper and "it just so happened" that Kristy loved hanging wallpaper and had done it many times. So, again, we set a day, and she came up and taught us how to match it and hang it! And even started it for us by hanging some strips (we know that was part of God's plan)! The next few days, Katy and I hung wallpaper. Then we put the beautiful border along to cover where the wallpaper met the paint.

Archie came along, and in approving the room, so far said, "I have an extra piece of pink carpet that will fit this room. I think it's the same shade of pink as the flowers in the border."

So, we went to his house, and sure enough, his "extra" carpet would work! We got it to our house, and lo and behold, it WAS THE EXACT SAME PINK as in some of the flowers! We laid it down and it just set the room off perfectly (there is God again)!

Then a couple of weekends later, Sam, a friend of ours, came to visit and he brought another friend, Scott from Georgia.

Are you ready for this? I did not realize this before, but Sam is a carpet layer by trade. We bought the metal edging and they (Sam and Scott) stretched the carpet and laid it professionally (there's God again!)

My son, Dallas, had an extra ceiling fan that he gave us that had four separate lights: one night-light at the top and three lights hanging down. All the lights had stained glass globes around them with some of them the same colors as the wallpaper and border. Another of God's blessings!

The room that was built on for a dining room wasn't finished either. Just watch and see how God worked this room all out too!

My daughter-in-law's (Susanna) brother, Jonathan, lays tile. So, he came one day and laid the tile (that God helped us get for the dining room floor) professionally.

The ceiling in the dining room would not hold paint, so I did not know quite how to do the ceiling. One day, Dallas said, "Ask Archie's father. He's the best with ceilings that I know." So, I phoned Archie's dad. He said on the phone, "Do you have some mud?" (Meaning sheet rock mud.) It just so happened there was a half of a five-gallon bucket left over from putting up the sheet rock. So, I said, "Yes." (Another miracle.)

He said, "Do you have a plastic bag?"

I said, "Yes."

He said, "OK, I'll do it."

The day he could do it was decided. He came up and started up the ladder with the two things he had asked for. Right then, the telephone rang, and I ran to answer it. When I got back, he was done already with the ceiling and coming back down the ladder. I didn't even get to watch him. He did a beautiful job on the ceiling (God's arrangement again)!

My son, Dallas, worked for a contractor, building beautiful houses. One day, while he was at work, a lady who owned the house they were just finishing came out of her new house with lots of what looked like material draped over her arm. And said to all the workers there, "These drapes that I made do not fit in these windows. Does anyone want them before I throw them into the dumpster?" (There's God again!)

Dallas said, "Yes, I want them."

She gave them to Dallas, He put them in his car. Later that evening, he brought them home and gave them to me. They were beautiful! Pink with white lining; the same shade of pink as the parlor carpet and the same pink as the flowers in the wallpaper border! They matched perfectly! And they fit our dining room windows perfectly! (See God working again?) There were three walls in the dining room, because the fourth wall was all open into the parlor. A regular-sized window was on the back side, facing the woods; a long, floor-to-ceiling window was on another wall, facing the side yard. The third was a whole blank white wall.

Katy and I always seated our guests at the table with their backs to the blank wall—so they could see out one of the windows while we ate and not where they had to face the blank wall. One day, Katy said, "Why don't we put a mural on the blank wall, so we can seat people facing any direction, and not have to worry about someone facing a blank wall?"

We prayed about it, and both of us went together to look for a mural. God showed us a wallpaper store that had a good selection of murals. They showed us to a mural book to look through to make our selection, and sure enough, there was the perfect mural for our wall! It was a picture of a half opened French door leading out into a beautiful flower garden, with a stone walkway leading through the flowers to an arched trellis, complete with a little bunny rabbit sitting right down in the middle of the flowers. We purchased that one and took it home. Together we hung it on the wall, and it looked very real. In fact, it looked so real that one day, after we got it up on the wall, we saw a little bug flying in the dining room. It kept flying into the wall where the open-door part of the picture was, trying to fly to the outside. There is our awesome God again! I had no idea that bugs could see that big of a spectrum!

Clarence donated his beautiful antique floor lamp for the parlor. His aunt had crocheted a lacy lamp shade and starched it stiff to hang down over the pink light bulb. It was soo pretty and perfect for the parlor. Also Clarence brought up his beautiful chandelier to hang from the middle of the ceiling above the dining room table (there is God prompting again).

God had provided the perfect décor to make our drab, plain rooms pretty and cozy in which to live and entertain our friends and family. And it was also inexpensive. None of those precious people that helped us would let us pay them! They were truly sent by God.

We had many, many celebrations in our home after that: birthdays, graduations, special events, many, many parties to encourage people and show them they were loved. We had my daddy's ninetieth birthday celebration, where over sixty people came (a come and go party).

We had room for ten people to sleep at our house at a time, and of course, eat there too. We had many people throughout the years (some that we had just met) that needed a place to stay for a few days or months or years. God helped us to get it all fixed nice and then use it for His honor and glory to help people.

We serve such an awesome God! He loves beauty! Just think how He made and decorated our world with so many kinds, colors, sizes, and fragrances of just flowers alone. Not to mention all the different trees, bushes, grasses, streams of water, lakes, ponds, and touched it all off with not just one bunny rabbit but many and all kinds, shapes, sizes, and colors of animals too. That's just what we can see on the surface. There's also lots more underwater, and in space, to see if we venture there.

God definitely loves beauty! He made all of US too! All of this because He loves YOU and ME! What do you say? Let's love Him back—enough to obey Him! OK?

Jesus Bids Us Shine

Susan Warner, 1868

Edwin Othello Excell

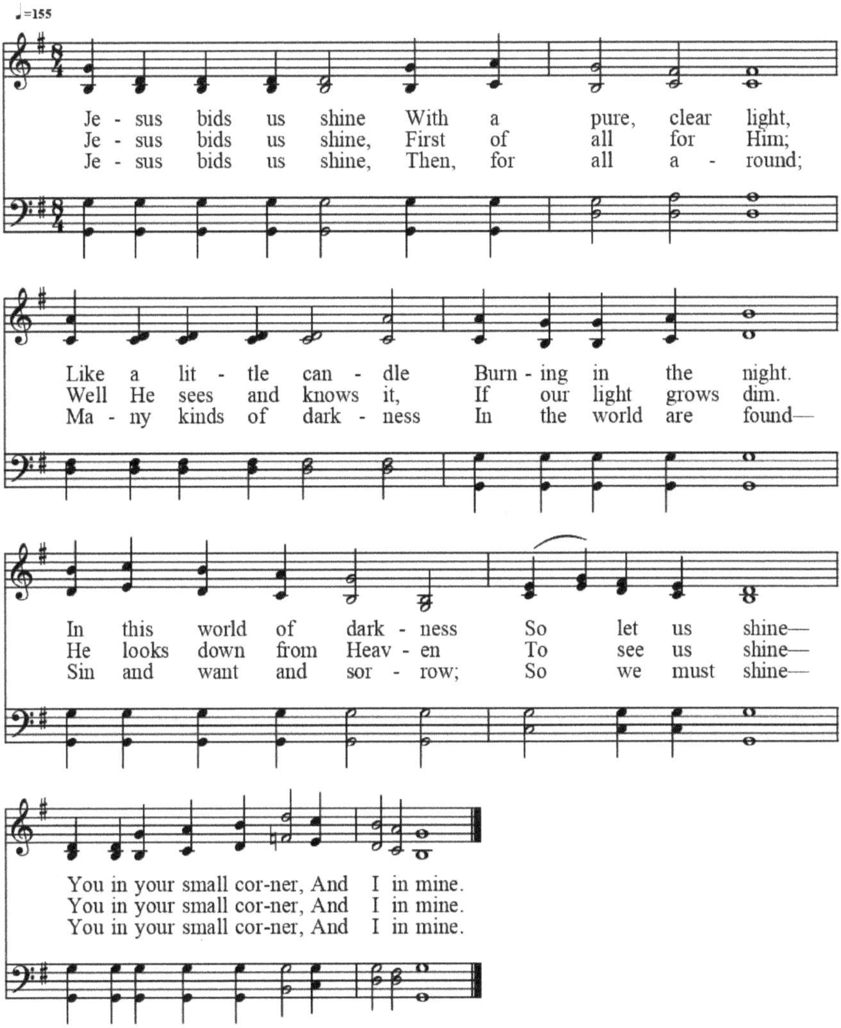

The Table

One day, someone gave us a coffee table. It was the most beautiful table I had ever seen. The table was clear glass, so you could see from the top the beautiful golden legs holding it up from underneath. The table was oval shape, about three feet long and about a foot and a half across the top at the widest part. It had four very sturdy wooden spiral-shaped legs on each end, painted a beautiful gold color from the glass down to the crescent-shaped base on the floor, about two inches apart, and a crescent shape at each end of the table. It was just perfect for our new parlor. It sat right in front of the green upholstered loveseat. I knew God had worked that out for our new parlor too. But it WAS just a piece of furniture.

But in my estimation, it was the prettiest, most valuable piece of furniture that I owned. I loved it too much. I dusted it regularly and took such good care of it. The only thing I allowed on it was a vase of a dozen red or champagne-colored roses or whatever color flowers people gave to me from time to time. I did not allow anyone to put anything else on it at any time, except when we had our Bible studies with different people, and they laid their Bibles on the pretty table. Thankfully, I allowed that! The most important book on MY important table.

Some years later, I had a patient with dementia. She was so precious. I just loved her. We got along so well. She almost always slept through the night. If she DID wake up at night, she always stayed in her room. Every time throughout the night, when I checked on my patients, she was sleeping. She had the cutest little hum when she was walking around during the day. My bedroom (the other new room that my husband and son had built) was through a single door off of the parlor on the opposite side from the dining room. There was another doorway that came from the front part of the house into the parlor.

One night, I woke up to that soft, sweet little hum. As I was waking up, I was thinking, *Oh, how sweet, she's up humming.* But then, wide awake, I realized, *Hey, it's the middle of the night and she's up and in the parlor. What is she doing in there?* I was just jumping out of bed when *CRASH*! My little patient fell on my coffee table. Instantly, I was by her side, helping her up. Thankfully, she was OK, and I helped her back to bed. The table "seemed" OK too.

A few nights later, this happened again, then again, and later again. This went on for six weeks. Thankfully, my patient was OK, and the table seemed OK but seemed to be getting a tad wobbly now.

The sixth week, my patient got up and came and fell on it, and my pride and joy coffee table crumbled to the floor in many pieces. Thankfully then, my patient was not hurt. That was a miracle in itself. But my coffee table was ruined, in too many pieces to be fixed. Strangely enough, the glass itself did not break, but the golden legs were shattered in many, many pieces.

I am ashamed to say, for a brief moment I had resentment toward my patient. But almost immediately God impressed on me that this happened because of ME. I had made a god out of that pretty table that He Himself had given me, because I had put that table before Him and was selfishly stingy with its use, affecting other people in the wrong way. And I even had held resentment toward my patient, who is a human being that God loves and died for.

I then helped her up, checked her all over to make sure she was OK, gave her a big hug, and helped her back to bed. My patient never got up and went into the parlor again at night.

I know God allowed that to happen to teach me to love Him, not things. People are *always* more important than things.

I cleaned up the mess of all the hundreds of pieces of splintered wood stuck in the carpet and prayed that God would forgive me and help me to never put anything or anyone between Him and me again.

"Thou shalt have no other gods before me" (Exod. 20:3). HIS FIRST LAW!

The Flirt

My daughter, Katy, had finished her three college courses in evangelism, food service directors program, and allied health, and was preparing for graduation from the school she was attending, just fifteen miles south of Rapid City, South Dakota. After that, she was planning to drive her Jeep Wrangler back home to North Carolina. So, I decided to surprise her for her graduation. I planned to take the Greyhound Bus out to South Dakota for her graduation and then also to drive back with her in the Jeep, so she wouldn't have to drive the 1,600+ miles all by herself.

I got the road atlas out and called to get the bus schedules all together and planned the whole trip to be able to make the bus changes on time. The whole trip ended up taking fifty hours (this is the same trip from Book 2—where God had me meet "The 'Mean' Girl").

A bus change and a few hours later (after that divine encounter), further into the trip, the bus I was on now pulled into a station in Sioux City, Iowa, about 10:00 at night.

I knew this was another place to change buses, so I waited for my luggage to be unloaded, then took it all inside to look at the schedule to see when the next bus would leave. What I did not know in planning my trip was that this particular station closes down at night, and everyone goes home. Right after my bus arrived, and I got inside the bus station, the gift shop closed, the little café closed, the ticket agent started turning off lights and locking doors. I asked him, "Where should I wait and catch my next bus?"

He looked at my ticket and said, "Oh, that one is the first one to leave here tomorrow morning at 8:30. You can wait here in the lobby; I leave the bathrooms unlocked. Good night." And he was gone too.

The people that had gotten off of my bus had all gone home too, except for two men that had made themselves comfortable on opposite sides of the little station.

Shocked, I stood there not knowing quite what to do. I sent up a little prayer to God, asking Him to show me what to do about this situation. The seats in the lobby were narrow and each one had stationary arm rests on both sides of them. They were all connected in rows, so there was no way to lie down or lean back very far. The backs were straight up and down. So there I was for the whole night, in a small bus station with two men who were complete strangers to me and nowhere to even put up my feet for the next ten hours.

This was the end of November, and it was already really cold outside, so I decided to be very thankful and to dwell on the fact that I could be nice and warm indoors with the heat.

Over in one corner, close to the diner, I saw a couple of tables with chairs, so I took my luggage over there and sat down on one of the chairs, put my purse in my lap with my coat over it, and arranged all my suitcases around me. That way, I could lay my head over on the table, with one arm under my head and the other arm draped across my suitcases and catch a wink of sleep.

Sometime in the wee hours of the morning, around 2:00 a.m., I woke up for the umpteenth time, only this time unable to go back to sleep, being so uncomfortable. I looked around and accounted for both of the men. I stood up to change my position and decided to walk around a bit within sight of my luggage. I walked over to the closed gift shop and peered in the window at the pretty things.

Suddenly, I was aware of someone close behind me! Just then a male voice said something flirty about me being pretty. Without me flinching or being afraid, God bypassed my mind and out of my mouth came, "Thank you; God made me that way."

The man, now standing in front of me (I'll call him John), said, "Oh! I don't believe in God."

At that very moment, God helped my heart go out to him; he looked so sad and discouraged. I said, "Oh, how come you don't believe in God?"

John's eyes started watering as he said, "My wife just left me; my kids have disowned me; I just lost my job; then they came and picked up my car 'cause I couldn't make the payments, and now my mother just died. If there's a God and He is so good and merciful, why is He doing all of this to me?"

I said, "Oh, bless your heart! I am so very sorry you have gone through all of this." I told him that "God doesn't CAUSE bad things to happen to people, because God *is* good and loves all of His people that He has made and loves us all the same. But He ALLOWS trials to come to people for various reasons.

"What do you mean?" he asked.

"Sometimes, it's not something that we ourselves have caused, but sometimes it's because of our own wrong decisions and actions that we bring these things on ourselves. But either way, God is still there, protecting us from the worst. He allows us to see our wrong actions and wants to help us change them IF WE WILL LET HIM. But if we persist in doing things our own way and refuse to obey the God that dearly loves us, then finally, He will leave us alone to do what we ourselves want to do. But if we realize we need help and ask God to help us, He will!"

I told him about Job in the Bible and all the trials he went through and how Job's "friends" and even his wife tried to get him to turn against God.

"Just like you, John, Job lost his job; his wife basically turned against him for a time, and he lost all of his children too—except his children were all killed [Job chapters 1 and 2]. But because Job refused to turn his back on God and chose rather to stick with God, the Bible says that God repaid Job with more and more blessings. God vindicated Job and doubly recompensed Job [Job chapter 42]."

"We don't always have to know the exact reason for our trials, though we can know for a certainty that when all you have left is God, then for the first time you realize that God is enough. Remember, John, 'True peace is not necessarily the absence of trouble, but true peace is ALWAYS the presence of God.' If your trials bring you and your relatives, friends, or anyone, closer to God, then they are worth it."

"If the mountain we are climbing doesn't have curves, bumps, rocks, and jagged places to get a foothold, if it is totally smooth, we would slip and slide and could NEVER get to the top."

"All the trials that come to God's people come through Jesus first. That means that Jesus picks and chooses what you and He together can handle. Not you, John, by yourself, but you and God TOGETHER."

"Remember, John, God is ALWAYS there and will help you IF you let Him. Turn to Him, cling to Him, let Him work in your life."

By now, John was crying! He said, "I want Him in my life. How can I have Him?"

I answered, "Just ask Him," and was going to continue to explain how to ask Him and how Jesus wants to draw us to Him and give us salvation, but we didn't realize that we had talked the whole rest of the night, because just then, in came the ticket agent unlocking the doors and people started pouring into the lobby of the bus station. I looked at the clock: it was 7:30 in the morning already!

It got super noisy with all the other passengers in there talking around us, to the point that John and I were almost yelling to be able to hear each other. Still sobbing uncontrollably, he grabbed my arm and said loudly, above the noise, "Please don't leave me until you tell me how to get Him."

Loudly, straight to him, I said back, "We can't talk in here. Let's go outside," as I took his arm and gently led him in and out through the crowd of people that had gathered toward the door to the outside.

There on the small porch at the top of the steps, we found a small spot behind the open glass doors. I said, "Let's pray to God and ask Him to come into your heart right now and to forgive your sins and to help you to see Him working in your life."

John looked around at all the people going by and looking at us, and said, "Here? Now? But the people can still see us and me crying."

I said, "Yes, and it's OK; they don't matter right now," pointing toward the people.

I prayed first, and then John prayed—slowly and childlike, begging God to come in and take over his life. During the prayer, John quit crying and a peace seemed to totally embrace him ("Thou wilt keep him in perfect peace, whose mind is stayed on thee: because he trusteth in thee." Isaiah 26:3).

As he finished his short but sincere prayer, the crowd of people still flocking into the station were now pushing the glass doors against us as more and more people at a time were going through the doors, so we had to move again.

As we parted, John was saying, "Thank you! Thank you! Thank you for talking to me, explaining, and helping me to see the truth about God!" As the growing crowd of people engulfed us, I told him I would keep praying for him.

Of course, I never saw him again, but I still pray for him. I pray that he was able to obtain a Bible and learn more of God's promises that even though all of us have sinned, God loves us all so very much that He forgives us IF we ask and do our best to turn away from our sins, and other Bible verses explaining more about salvation and how God wants to be our God and wants us to be HIS people:

1. The Lamb of God—takes away sin. John 1:29, "The next day John seeth Jesus coming unto him, and saith, Behold the Lamb of God, which taketh away the sin of the world."

2. We are all sinners—we need what Jesus does. Romans 3:23, "For all have sinned, and come short of the glory of God."

3. Forgiveness and cleansing are assured to the repentant. 1 John 1:9, "If we confess our sins, he is faithful and just to forgive us our sins, and to cleanse us from all unrighteousness."

4. The law is written on our heart—heart obedience. Jeremiah 31:33, "But this shall be the covenant that I will make with the house of Israel; after those days, saith the LORD, I will put my law in their inward parts, and write it in their hearts; and will be their God, and they shall be my people."

5. Power to become children of God. John 1:12, "But as many as received him, to them gave he power to become the sons of God, even to them that believe on his name."

6. Believe to righteousness—confess to salvation. Romans 10:10, "For with the heart man believeth unto [resulting in] righteousness; and with the mouth confession is made unto salvation."

7. Heart obedience. 1 John 2:3–6, "And hereby we do know that we know him, if we keep his commandments. He that saith, I know

him, and keepeth not his commandments, is a liar, and the truth is not in him. But whoso keepeth his word, in him verily is the love of God perfected: hereby know we that we are in him. He that saith he abideth [lives] in him ought himself also so to walk, even as he walked."

8. Children of God—like Jesus. 1 John 3:1–2, "Behold, what manner of love the Father hath bestowed upon us, that we should be called the sons [children] of God: therefore the world knoweth us not, because it knew him not. Beloved, now are we the sons of God, and it doth not yet appear what we shall be: but we know that, when he shall appear, we shall be like him; for we shall see him as he is."

Obedience does not earn salvation but it is the glad-hearted response of love to Christ for what He has done to forgive our sins and make salvation available to us.

Isn't that exciting, dear friend, to know that even though some people spend a lifetime looking for and searching out their gods, and trying to appease them, that OUR God, the God who made heaven and earth, comes looking for us, trying to draw us back to Him. Isn't our God awesome?! That bus station experience could have been unnerving, being locked inside a bus station lobby with two men I had never seen before, all the telephones locked up in offices (no cell phones back then, of course), and I was not sure how to handle that type of comment, but God bypassed my mind and had the words, "thank you, God made me this way" come straight out of my mouth, immediately bringing God into the conversation.

I'm so thankful for all He is teaching me. We sure serve an awesome God!

The Addiction

My children and I almost never watched TV when they were young. We always had so many more things to do, like doing chores, playing out in the yard or the woods, playing games, or doing puzzles. Also, we loved to learn how to cook together and had many sewing projects together. But after Dallas started school, peer pressure entered the picture. His classmates would come to school on any morning saying things like, "Man! Did you see that program last night?" Or "Wow! Did you see [an actor or actress] last night—what [he or she] did?"

Of course, little Dallas had nothing to talk about in that line of conversation. All he had done was his household duties, play games, catch crawdads in the creek behind our house, go hiking with his family and other friends, play with his sister, and/or make greeting cards to take to "shut-ins" that we visited and other things like that.

So, one day, when he came home from school, he said, "Mommy, can we watch something on television, so I will have something to talk about when Bobby and Tommy and the others are talking about their TV programs?"

I had just read a few days before something that said when you take something away from a child that is not good for them, then you should replace it with something that IS good for them.

So, I thought, *OK, we could go to the video store and check out a children's video for Saturday night (our game and family time together on Saturday nights). That way we hopefully could pick something better for us to watch.* (It would be many years before I realized that this was NOT a good replacement but was actually a bad decision.) So, on Friday, while Dallas was in school, I went to a video store and checked out one that I thought was appropriate for children. Interestingly enough, when little Dallas went to school on Monday morning talking about the cute, non-violent movie we had watched on Saturday night, the other children had never seen it before. They asked many questions and made comments like, "I wish I could see that one," or "Can I come to your house and see that one?"

So began a new tradition in our home. Some Saturday nights, we still played games and read stories and did other fun things together. But more and more we got into the movies until I, for one, was hooked. My friend Ginger and her three children often came over on Saturday nights to eat supper and watch our video (usually one I remembered from childhood).

By the time my children were entering their teen years, we had many, many of our own copies of movies.

I was one of the room mothers for both of my children's school classes, so when Dallas got to the eighth grade, I wanted to do something special for him and each of his classmates for their eighth grade graduation.

I decided before school started that year that I would make each one a decorative pillow in their favorite colors with their name on it. After they would make their bed, they would be able to put their personalized pillow on their bed. I designed each pillow to be a little over a foot square with their name punched in yarn, caddy corner across one side from corner to corner, and big squares of their favorite color combinations on the other side, complete with long tassels on each corner. Each pillow took five hours to make, including the yarn punching.

Each day, when I was at home and the kids were at school, I worked on pillows after all my house and garden work was done. So, what did I do while I was sewing? I would put on one of the movies that we had collected through the years. Sadly, I became addicted to five of the non-children movies. Through the 190–200 hours of sewing pillows all through that school year, I am ashamed to say that I watched some of those movies thirty to thirty-five times each.

Of course, it was during the day when no one else was home. I did the pillows as a surprise for Dallas, Katy, and all the students—and did it again for Katy's eighth grade class. I loved to sew; it was all so fun. That part was good. But feeding my new addiction was NOT so good.

When my last child graduated from high school and was planning to go away to college, I was trying to adjust my mind to the fact that I would be alone on Friday and Saturday nights. So, I immediately started planning what I would do each of those nights after my daughter left to keep myself happy and in a good frame of mine. Friday night was no problem, of course, because at sundown on Friday to sundown on Saturday is the Bible Sabbath. I could read my Bible and spend quality time talking with my best friend, Creator, and redeemer, Jesus. I love doing that.

But on Saturday night after sundown, I decided that I would watch one movie each week of my favorite popular singer. He had made many movies back then, and I had not seen all of them yet. So, I thought that would be fun. The first Saturday night, all alone and after sundown, I put my sweater on to go to the video store to check out one of his movies. I was leaving home at 8:20 p.m., walking toward the front door, when all of a sudden, the desire to watch his movie left me.

I didn't know why. I took off my sweater, went to my room, changed my clothes, and went to bed. To my shock, I never had a desire to watch that singer's movies again. (I did not understand why this happened until a month or so later.) On Saturday nights, for many years after that, I read my Bible and had people over for supper and Bible study groups.

Sometime later after that Saturday night, Katy and I were talking, and she told me about her friend, Rudy, a new minister of the gospel that she met at college. He and Katy were hiking in the mountains together close to Black Hills, South Dakota, that same Sabbath afternoon. He asked about her parents. Katy told him her dad was a truck driver. Rudy then asked, "Is he able to guard the edges of the Sabbath?" (In other words—the Bible says that Sabbath is from sundown on Friday, the sixth day, until sundown on Saturday, the seventh day. So, rather than doing our own thing right up until sundown and then trying to switch our mind over at the last minute at sundown to Sabbath thoughts and our Holy God/Jesus, we should prepare our mind ahead of time to think of God and His love, His nature, His mercy, and His law; so, we are already in the Sabbath mode before Sabbath actually starts at sundown. That's what Rudy meant by "guarding the edges of the Sabbath.")

Because driving a commercial truck, Katy's dad sometimes could pull over early on Friday to prepare for Sabbath like at a truck stop or a pretty park, Katy answered, "Well sometimes he does guard the edges."

Rudy said, "Well, let's pray right now for him that he can for today and always guard the edges of the Sabbath."

Right then, Rudy and Katy came to a big flat rock beside their hiking trail and knelt down right then on that big rock, and Rudy prayed for Katy's dad, and in the prayer, he also prayed for Katy's mother—ME! (It was Sabbath afternoon at 6:20 p.m.) He did not know me. He did not know that right that minute, I had just put on my sweater to go out the door to check out a movie of what was then my favorite popular worldly singer. (When it is 6:20 p.m. mountain time where they were, it is 8:20 p.m. eastern time where I lived.)

Rudy had no idea that his fervent prayer took away forever my desire to watch that singer's movies. Isn't that what intercessory prayer is? Praying for other people.

WOW! See how important intercessory prayer is! Rudy prayed that prayer for me 2,000 + miles away from where I was at the time, but it took effect THAT VERY SAME MOMENT!

So, dear reader, KEEP PRAYING for whoever you are praying for anywhere in the world. "The effectual fervent prayer of a righteous man availeth [accomplishes] much" (James 5:16).

The rest of my addiction still lingered until one night God gave me a dream. In this dream, I was at my house, but the house was different. There was a huge, long picture window all across one wall of the living room from the ceiling to halfway down the wall about waist high, looking out across the yard to a forest of trees. Inside, across the long narrow living room, opposite the picture window was a sofa against a solid wall. On this sofa sat a very good-looking man, nicely dressed, with his arms folded across his chest, leaning back against the back of the sofa. His legs were straight out in front of him, crossed at the ankles with his feet on the floor. He had a very nice smile. I sat beside him, talking to him, and occasionally giving him a big hug.

Lots of people were rushing back-and-forth between us and the picture window, rushing from the room at one end of the living room to the room at the other end of the living room, where the outside door was. They were talking and in a big hurry, preparing for the big storm.

At times, different ones would look at me on the couch, and say, "Rita, you'd better hurry!" Sometimes another one would say, "Rita, you'd better hurry and get ready for the storm; it's almost here!"

Now and then, I would get up from the couch and go over to the picture window to see the storm. The first time I looked out, the trees were barely moving. Later, when I got up and left my "good friend" on the couch and peered out of the picture window across at the trees, they were blowing more intensely. I knew a storm was coming, but then I would turn around and see that good-looking guy and my mind would go back to him. Smiling at him, I immediately hurried back to the couch, sat down, and continued hugging on him.

The crowd of people got less and less as THEY finished getting ready for the storm and going to the place of safety.

The last young lady, as she passed by us for the last time, said, in alarm, "Rita, hurry! You'd better get ready for the storm! COME ON!" And disappeared out the door at the opposite end of the living room.

I got up and went across the living room to the picture window and looked out. The storm was so bad now that the trees were bent all the way over in the strong winds. Again, I turned around to look at the good-looking guy. He never moved. He still sat the same way with his beautiful, alluring smile. His eyes always looking straight ahead, never at me, his arms always folded. I was the one loving and hugging on him. He never did put his arms around me.

Still, I turned my back on the storm, left the window, and headed back toward him. Then I woke up.

Immediately, God put into my mind that the man on the couch represented the movies I watched all the time. They were so very good-looking to me, and I loved them dearly. They did NOT love me back, but I loved them sooo much that I was putting them before and above everything else, including studying my Bible and spending time with my God, getting ready for the end of time and His second coming!

As you know, when God is trying to teach you something, He can send it from many different directions. So, one day I was watching Pastor Doug Batchelor on the Amazing Facts TV channel, when he said something like, "If you have in your house any magazines, DVDs, CDs, papers, books, records, or anything like that that are NOT pointing you to heaven, then Satan has a foothold in your home."

WOW! That really scared me! I definitely did NOT want Satan in my home at all! So, I brought in some empty boxes and started loading up our movies. I hauled them out of my house as quick as I could. I counted them as I packed and discovered that we had collected eighty-three movies through the years. Today, as I am writing this, thinking about what Doug Batchelor had said, I am thinking of other ways Satan could have a foothold in our homes. Now, we have the Internet where we can download movies, books, and songs onto our computers, laptops, tablets, or phones. We must be very careful what is being downloaded, watched, or listened to on our devices. They can either point us to Jesus or away from Him.

Just think how that "little" habit of watching "innocent" movies snowballed with me until it took up the majority of my mind! After I was convicted to get rid of movies and secular music, etc., a friend called and wanted to come up and watch a movie one Saturday night. I had two DVDs of India. Each had nine fifteen-minute programs talking about the loving people of India and their culture, so when my friend got there, I told her about those, and she said, "Let's watch one of the fifteen-minute programs."

They were so interesting and informative that she wanted to watch another one and another. We ended up watching all eighteen of them that night. So, God had provided right then a replacement to help break my addiction. I am so very thankful for God showing me in time to change. Think of all the wasted time I spent filling my mind with foolish thoughts that were taking me away from God when I could have been using that time to study my Bible, pray, and learn how to prepare for heaven myself. And how to help other people to be ready for Jesus' second coming! He literally took that very strong desire away that I had developed for years.

We sure serve an awesome God!

Jesus Bids Us Shine

Public Domain
Courtesy of the Cyber Hymnal™

The Cookies

My daughter, Katy, was living in Loma Linda, California, when she was called to go to Guam to be a doctor of physical therapy and to help teach the medical evangelism class. They called her from Guam on a Thursday. She told them she needed time to pray about it. Three days later, on Sunday, she called me on the phone in Fletcher, North Carolina, and said, "Mother, I've been praying about this; God wants me to go to Guam, and I want YOU to go with me."

"Guam? Where is Guam?" I answered, totally shocked.

"Mother, get your world atlas out and look up Guam."

So, I did. I finally found it, a teeny, tiny little dot in the middle of the huge Pacific Ocean. Then, I picked the receiver back up and anxiously said, "Katy, we can't both go! We will sink it!" I didn't think I wanted to go to a "dot" in the ocean.

Katy pleaded. I kept thinking of reasons NOT to go. Two days later, early Tuesday morning, my friend, Allene, called and was asking how all my family was doing. When she got to Katy, I said, "Katy's moving to Guam." Allene immediately came back with, "And you are going with her, aren't you?"

I said, "Well, no."

That's all I got out of my mouth. For the next forty-five minutes, Allene yelled continuously at me, starting out with, "What do you mean, no? Of course you are going with her! You have no business staying here by yourself when your daughter wants you with her." And on and on and on.

While Allene was loudly voicing her opinion, I remembered something Katy had told me herself a couple of years before, when I was having a hard time prayerfully deciding which way to do something. Katy said, "Mother, God hates indecision. Pick one way that you think God wants you to take and do that. Then if it's not the right way, HE will close the door. You accept that and go with the other choice you had."

> *"Mother, I've been praying about this; God wants me to go to Guam, and I want YOU to go with me." "Guam? Where is Guam?" I answered, totally shocked.*

So, I thought, *OK, I'll choose to go to Guam, and if God doesn't want me to go to Guam, He will close the door.*

And so now, with Allene "encouraging" me to go with Katy, I decided to go. So, when Allene slowed down a bit and stopped to take a breath, I said, "OK, Allene, I'll go."

She was so relieved! And I am thankful for her "yelling" at me that way to get my attention and so very thankful to get to go to Guam, because I love Guam and the people here. (Nine years ago, I came back to Guam after a brief period in the States and am loving every minute!) God is blessing the island very much. Sometimes I see three to five rainbows a week: single, double, and even triple. Do we ever take time to think about the pretty rainbow and what it REALLY means?

> Lest the gathering clouds and falling rain should fill men with constant terror, from fear of another flood, the Lord encouraged the family of Noah [including us, today] by a promise: 'I will establish My covenant with you; ... neither shall there any more be a flood to destroy the

earth.... I do set My bow in the cloud, and it shall be for a token of a covenant between Me and the earth. And it shall come to pass, when I bring a cloud over the earth, that the bow shall be seen in the cloud.... And I will look upon it, that I may remember the everlasting covenant between God and every living creature.' [Gen. 9:11–16.] How great the condescension of God and His compassion for His erring creatures in thus placing the beautiful rainbow in the clouds as a token of His covenant with men! The Lord declares that when He looks upon the bow, He will remember His covenant. This does not imply that He would ever forget; but He speaks to us in our own language, that we may better understand Him. It was God's purpose that as the children of after generations should ask the meaning of the glorious arch which spans the heavens, their parents should repeat the story of the Flood, and tell them that the Most High had bended the bow and placed it in the clouds as an assurance that the waters should never again overflow the earth. Thus from generation to generation it would testify of divine love to man and would strengthen his confidence in God. (*Patriarchs and Prophets,* p. 106)

WOW! Learning that helps us to love and appreciate the rainbow even more, doesn't it?

Now back to my Guam story.

While we were in Guam for those two plus years, we had eleven typhoons. Most of them did little or no damage. We were all praying with each typhoon, and I know that God really blesses this little dot in the Pacific Ocean. I remember one full category 5 typhoon that came right up to Guam, stopped, went backwards away from Guam, and came again north of Guam, not hitting Guam at all!

Another category 5 typhoon split, with the eye of the typhoon going right along the edge of our island. The top part of the storm, above the eye, was over the ocean and the other islands, tearing everything up in its path, while the bottom part of that same typhoon that was over our island was like the level of a tropical storm, with minimum wind and rain, and didn't destroy anything. I remember the weather forecasters on the radio and television saying that they had never seen a split typhoon before.

Right there are three ways out of the "thousand ways" that God can take care of His people (*The Desire of Ages,* p. 330).

At that time, I worked for JOYFM radio station and had two programs a week on the radio myself. So, after each of the miracle typhoons, God helped me remind the listeners of His miracles and His love and protection for us.

The worst typhoon that we had in those two plus years that we were in Guam was called Dolphin. It hit on a Friday afternoon, right when we were trying to finish our housework by sundown for Sabbath. The winds got up to 106 miles per hour; the power over most of the island went off at 4:30 p.m., and the power crew went off duty at 5:00 p.m. because of the danger, so they were not available to restore the power. The island power was off through the night. But God, in His mercy, brought the power back on five different times through the night, each time for about half an hour or so. So, we didn't lose any food in the refrigerator or freezer.

That Friday afternoon, when Dolphin hit, Katy was making three trays of cookies for a special occasion. She had just gotten one tray of cookies ready to bake when the power went off. She went ahead and put that tray in the already preheated oven, even though it was off now. Then she got the second tray all ready to put in the oven. Then, suddenly, the power came back on. So, she put the second tray into the oven. Then just as the soon as both trays were done, the power went off again. But the two trays were done! We were praying, of course, for protection from the storm and for the power to come back on. The power came back on right then, and the third tray of cookies got baked and then the power went off again for hours.

Isn't our God awesome?! He even cares about us getting our cookies baked before the Sabbath begins.

God really blesses this little dot in the ocean (this dot turns out to be thirty miles long and eight miles wide in the widest spot).

The Knot

We were in National Airport in Washington, DC, the time my son Dallas was leaving to go teach in Russia right after Communism had fallen (*God in My Life,* book 2). As I was crying because he was going SO far away to such an unknown situation, Dallas, who was eight inches taller than me, stood in front of me, took a hold of my shoulders looking down into my face and said, "Mommy, God can take just as good care of me in Russia as He can here in the United States."

Until that point, I had never thought about God being everywhere. Guess I must have thought that we had a monopoly on God or something here in the States. Anyway, now I was to learn that God is also in Guam.

One of the first things that happened after we arrived in Guam is that Katy ordered and received two of the polo shirts to wear for her job as the director of the Physical Therapy Department, with the department logo on them. Two was all she could afford at the time. She planned to wear one while the other was being washed, switching back and forth.

One day at work, the stitching on one of the polo shirts got caught on a sharp object and pulled the threads out. Wouldn't you know, it was right in the very front of the shirt, about halfway down, right where it shows the most.

My mother, Kate Crowder, and her sisters had specialized in being able to pull threads back through to the back side of the cloth so that you couldn't even tell anything was wrong with it from the front side. So, I tried to remember what she had taught me but to no avail. It's not like you could cut it and redo it; that would ravel and make a bigger hole.

Time and again, day after day, I tried to work on it, to pull it back through, trying to find the right tiny little thread that had been damaged. All this time, we were washing and drying out Katy's one good shirt each evening to wear the next day.

By now, with all the working on it for days trying to fix the shirt, the tangled knot in the thread of the front part of the shirt had gotten bigger and BIGGER until the tangle was a fourth of an inch big. Of course, that big of a knot could not possibly be pulled through the stitching to the back. It would have to be untangled, which by now was impossible.

Finally, one day I was so frustrated trying to untangle the knot that I was crying. I prayed, "God, what can I do? We don't have enough money to buy another shirt, and Katy can't wear this like it is. Please do something." I laid the shirt down in my lap as I was crying and praying.

I closed my eyes to wipe them, then reopened them and picked the shirt up again. The knot—that HUGE knot—was GONE! But where did it go? I turned the shirt to the wrong side and looked, and there was that big knot inside the shirt, right where I was trying to pull it to.

The outside front of the shirt was perfectly smooth, almost like brand new again. No noticeable trace of any rip in the stitching at all.

We serve an awesome God. He's all powerful; He's omnipresent; He's loving; He cares about us—even down to the stitching in our clothes.

WOW!!! WHAT A GOD!!!

Jesus said, "With men it is impossible, but not with God: for with God all things are possible" (Mark 10:27 and Matt. 19:26).

The Diet

As you know, if you have read the other books in this series, *God in My Life,* God has allowed many warnings to be given to me throughout my life to show me that "God means what He says." The most recent warning at this writing had to do with my ideas on diet—the way I was eating. And, as usual, I thought MY idea was correct, and since I thought it was correct, I just KNEW it had to be God's way too. So, of course, God had to "set me straight" again.

I am so thankful to Him for His patience and that He keeps working with me and hasn't given up on me yet.

I had the misconception that since I am eating totally vegan that I could eat all I want. "It's healthy food, so eat all you want," in spite of the fact that the Bible says NOT to overeat. The Bible calls it surfeiting (being out of control and overindulging, especially in eating) (Luke 21:34).

Well, through all those years of eating vegan, I continued to "pig out" and eat until I was stuffed, overeating even on the healthy foods. I was always overeating until I was stuffed and then even eating more because it was good, and I was craving it, even though I already knew that overeating causes lots of taxation on the organs in our bodies.

For example, nuts! The whole time I had my own home health business, I carried a large Tupperware container in the car seat beside me full of my own homemade trail mix (large variety of nuts and dried fruits) as I dashed frantically to the next patient's house, gobbling handfuls of nuts as I drove, sometimes even eating the entire store-bought can full of nuts at a time. Sometimes, I had only two to five minutes to reach the next home of my six daily clients. So, I had to eat quickly enough so I could have a full meal before arriving at my next client's home.

In *Counsels on Diet and Foods*, page 363, God says through inspired counsel, "Care should be taken … not to use too large a proportion of nuts." The word sparingly is also used (p. 364). Nuts are very good for us, but we should eat them sparingly.

Sometimes that word "sparingly" would even come to my mind as I gobbled because God was gently reminding me. But I had already convinced myself that that "warning" did NOT mean me, because I was in a hurry and trying to make a living and take good care of these patients and do my best and on and on with the excuses.

But guess what, dear reader friend?! This law, this excellent and perfect advice, DOES MEAN ME! It means all of us—you and me. So back to my story.

Several years later, while I was still eating this way, my daughter Katy and her husband Atsushi, were living in Japan and received a call back to Guam as missionaries. Katy called me where I was living in Fletcher, North Carolina, to tell me, "We have been called back to Guam and after praying about it, we have accepted the call. We want you to come with us and help take care of Lumina. Could you do that?"

I prayed about it, and I said yes. How could Grandma ever turn down a request like that?! So, I joyfully made the trip to Guam too.

Atsushi accepted the position of director of nurses, and Katy teaches some classes and eight-week depression recovery courses for new clients as well as alumni programs for the graduates. Both Katy and Atsushi teach seminars on various subjects, such as medical assisting, Christian parenting, and how to give Bible studies, and do Bible studies themselves, and both fill in wherever needed in many other duties. Working for the

Lord, a person can "wear many hats." So, the busier Katy and Atsushi get, the more I get to take care of Lumina, now four years old.

One day, Ben, Cheryl and I had gone passing out literature on all three health aspects (mental, physical, and spiritual). We spent a couple of hours walking door to door in our neighborhood, enjoying the beautiful sunshine and walking up and down hills, having a wonderful time meeting people as we gave out information on how to better one's life.

I love doing this; it's one of my favorite activities to do. However, this was the first time to do this since my first heart attack eight years earlier (book 2, *GOD IN MY LIFE*). I did not realize, or even think about, the fact that my heart might not be up to this type of hot sun exertion yet.

The next morning, I ignored the fact of being super tired. Instead of asking for help, like I should do with what I THOUGHT had to be done, I picked up and moved the mattress off my double bed first and then picked up and moved the box spring off the bed frame, trying to arrange a large carpet/rug under my double bed.

Now, I DID ask for help. Atsushi came to my rescue, but by now I was feeling weak. The nausea started, and I laid down on one of the couches in the living room as the chest pain started.

Katy ran and got the cayenne pepper from the kitchen cabinet to stop the heart attack that seemed to be starting.

(After my first heart attack in my second book, *GOD IN MY LIFE*, Dallas had told us about cayenne pepper stopping heart attacks and strokes. So, two years later when I started having another heart attack, I laid down on the bed while Katy ran to the kitchen for cayenne powder and a spoon. Back in my room, she started spooning teaspoonfuls of cayenne into my mouth under my tongue, then into one side of my mouth, then into the other side, then straight into my mouth; she just kept spooning it in, as I was yelling, "Stop, Katy, stop!" as my mouth and tongue burned hotter and hotter. As she kept packing in the teaspoons full of the cayenne powder, Katy answered quickly, "But we don't know how much it takes!" That time the pain stopped in ten minutes, and the nausea went away. When I recovered from that incident, we again told Dallas about it. He was alarmed and said, "Well, you DON'T DO IT THAT WAY! You mix A LITTLE cayenne powder in some water and sip is SLOWLY!")

So, this time, like I said, we knew to do it the right way. To sip it slowly, and let it trickle down my throat using sips with a straw. After a couple of hours or so, the chest pain stopped, and the nausea went away. But still very weak, I rested the remainder of the day.

That was in November. The very next month in December, I went for my regularly scheduled checkup with my doctor. He had already ordered lab work which had already been done before the actual office visit.

Dr. Arnott had bad news and showed me the blood work report. All my numbers, including cholesterol, were high, especially my heart numbers. It showed I was very close to heart failure again. My heart could not take all the fat being stored. Yes, it was healthy fat, but because of my overeating, it was too much fat.

Some years before, I had a very good friend that died from her body storing her extra fat in her heart.

This doctor knew already that I do not take drugs. After showing me the alarming report, he got right in my face and said, "The only thing that is going to save your life is the therapeutic diet."

I said, "What is that?"

Backing up on his rolling stool, he said, "Train your mind to think bland, sour, tart, and some sweet. This is a 7 percent fat diet. What you can and should eat is:

1. Beans
2. Any and all 100 percent whole grains
3. Any and all vegetables (especially root vegetables). Yea! Potatoes are my favorite anyway.
4. Fruits

Then he said, "Eat all you want of these but no processed foods. But do eat two tablespoons of flax seed meal daily to get your daily fat intake."

Of course, this is somewhat like I had been telling and teaching people for years, since I had become vegan (fruits, grains, nuts, seeds, and vegetables).

What a shock! I thought I was "doing right," but my problem was not the healthy food itself, but the intemperance of overeating the healthy food.

While the doctor was so concerned, and talking so seriously to me, into my mind came God saying, "You have been teaching this to people for years, now I AM going to help you do it!"

What a thought! I loved it! Here was God helping me personally to overcome appetite: one of the main sins He has told us to avoid. The two hardest things to overcome, for us humans, are appetite and passion. Those who overcome appetite can overcome anything. I felt so close to God at that moment. That showed me right there that God is trying to prepare me for heaven if I will just let Him!

So, for the next three months, I ate only beans, whole grains, fruits, and vegetables. One of my favorite dishes became potatoes and carrots cooked together in water in a saucepan. Then as they got almost done, I would throw in some fresh broccoli to steam with them and a little salt. The three together are delicious.

This blood test and the results were in December of that year. Then, in March, I was tested again. To the joy of both my doctor and me, my numbers were all down, most of them to normal. Dr. Arnott was so excited, he was clapping his hands and squealing happily, as he said loudly, "And you did it without drugs! And you did it without drugs!" He was so excited! I was too, of course.

Dr. Arnott said my heart was out of danger for now, as long as I exercise daily To learn more, you can go to Dr. Arnott's website: drnewstart.com.

While this diet is good for bringing your numbers down, it should not be maintained longer than necessary.

Even after realizing some of what God was doing for me in all of this, the very next month, I slipped into compromising again.

I was still cooking the same vegan meals for my family through all this change, even though I was eating healthy differently than they were.

In April, after the super great test results in March, I decided on my own that "my heart is better so it's OK to 'taste' other things (that I'm not supposed to be eating for now), thinking, 'just a tiny little taste won't hurt anything.'" But God means what He says. Be moderate in all things, no overeating, no processed foods, for me, for now.

So, one day, I lifted a big spoonful of processed food that I was cooking for my family to my mouth to "taste" when a very strong voice impressed me saying, "I AM trying to bring you out of Sodom. *Pause.* DON'T...TURN...AROUND."

Wow! What a strong warning! It scared me. I started crying. To think that I was being like Lot's wife in the Bible (Luke 17:32; Gen. 19:15, 26) because she wasn't willing to give up her "precious" lifestyle for God. She turned to look back at what and who she was leaving rather than follow what God had shown her to save her life for eternity.

I put the spoonful of food down. I, too, was beginning to learn that God means what he says. I, too, need to be willing to give up ANYTHING for God, anything or anyone that stands between God and me.

I had lost thirty-three pounds in six months, and as long as I exercised, I was getting stronger, too. I pray every day now that God will help me to totally obey Him; that He will teach me His way and will lead me into all truth and that I will totally reflect His character.

God loves each one of us so very much! We all—you and me—need to spend more time with Him to show our love for Him, too. We need to spend at least one hour a day reading and contemplating (thinking about) Christ's life and love for us, including His death on the cross and His intercession for us going on now in heaven. Thank You, God and Jesus, for everything!

"I will praise thee; for I am fearfully and wonderfully made: marvellous are thy works; and that my soul knoweth right well" (Ps. 139:14).

O Love That Wilt Not Let Me Go

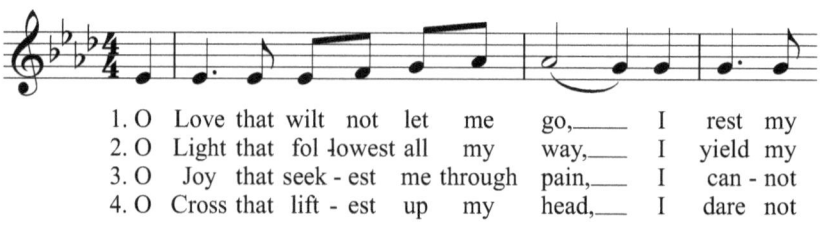

1. O Love that wilt not let me go, ⎯ I rest my
2. O Light that fol-lowest all my way, ⎯ I yield my
3. O Joy that seek-est me through pain, ⎯ I can-not
4. O Cross that lift-est up my head, ⎯ I dare not

wea-ry soul in thee;⎯ I give thee back the life I
flick'ering torch to thee;⎯ my heart re-stores its bor-rowed
close my heart to thee;⎯ I trace the rain-bow thru the
ask to fly from thee;⎯ I lay in dust life's glo-ry

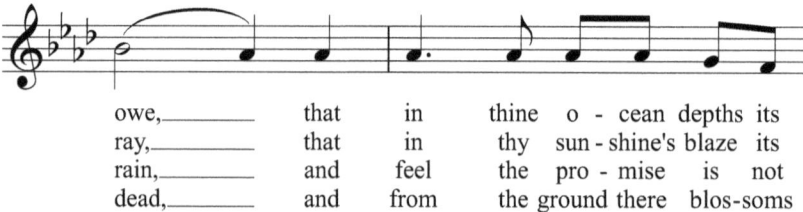

owe,⎯ that in thine o-cean depths its
ray,⎯ that in thy sun-shine's blaze its
rain,⎯ and feel the pro-mise is not
dead,⎯ and from the ground there blos-soms

flow may ri-cher, ful - ler be.
day may brigh-ter, fair - er be.
vain, that morn shall tear - less be.
red life that shall end - less be.

Hymnary.org

The Neatness Lesson

My newest granddaughter, Lumina (age three) loved helping to do everything. She helped make bread, tofu, entrees, cakes, and pies and other desserts. She liked to wash dishes and wipe the counters too. She loved to dust, vacuum, sweep, and mop the floors, in fact, she helped with most everything there was to do around the house.

She also loved to play on my bed. One day, I entered my bedroom to find papers of all kinds from off of my bedside table scattered all over the floor on one side of my bed. I said, very disappointed and frowning, "Oh, Lumina, NO!"

Sitting at the head of my bed, beside the bedside table, she looked at me with a big frown and puckered up ready to cry, so disappointed that I was disappointed in what she had done. Then, seconds later, she smiled really big and pointed to the perfectly cleaned off bedside table and said in hopeful tones, "Da?"

In other words, "But see, Grandma, the table is clean."

What a beautiful lesson I learned from my not-talking-yet granddaughter that day! "Grandma, keep clean and tidy—do NOT keep scattered papers out all over the furniture tops. Get organized and get the papers into files in the file cabinet drawers."

So, sure enough it hit me—yes, if I do not have papers out all over, then my little granddaughter can continue to play on my bed without having papers to throw all over the floor to clean off the bedside table top.

Now she can play on my bed with her felts and artificial food items without having to "help" clean up Grandma's stuff first. A good lesson for me to learn.

Our God is a God of organization.

"Let all things be done decently and in order" (1 Cor. 14:40).

"For God is not the author of confusion, but of peace" (1 Cor. 14:33).

> God is not glorified by those whom He has called out of darkness into His marvelous light being untidy, careless, and slovenly [sloppy].

We want to copy the heavenly Pattern as far as order and neatness are concerned, and, if heaven is desirable and attractive, I want that my premises shall be attractive in their simplicity and order. We all need to consider that thoroughness, neatness, and order should prevail among those who love and fear God, for in this we are recommending our faith.... Our connection with God will increase our desire to be cleanly in our houses and about our premises. (*This Day With God*, p. 331)

The Law

I must tell you one of the ideas that my daddy had and carried out during his last year of life.

As you know, if you read it from the second volume of *GOD IN MY LIFE*, my daddy, Amos Crowder, was very active and healthy but fell and fractured his back. Even though that put him in a wheelchair for a time, his mind was still very active. In his nineties, he still did not sit around doing nothing.

One day, he and I drove from Fletcher, North Carolina, to Collegedale, Tennessee, a suburb of Chattanooga, to spend a few days with Katy, his granddaughter. While there, a friend of his that lived in that area and had been a coworker from his working years in Orlando, Florida, came over to visit. Ed brought Daddy a beautiful poster of the Ten Commandments (God's law). It was eighteen inches long and fourteen inches wide, beautifully laminated, and had all the words to God's law as it is written in Exodus 20:3–17, not just one or two lines of each like sometimes quoted. (The law is also in Deuteronomy 5:7–21 and all throughout the Bible.)

Daddy loved the poster and asked Ed, "Where did you get this?" Ed told him. So, Daddy asked us to get him some posters to give out to his friends and others too.

When we got back to North Carolina, I called the number that Ed gave us, which turned out to be a business in Cleveland, Tennessee. I asked what quantity they came in and how much they cost. The man told me they were in bundles of 250 and were free!

I said, "FREE??"

He said, "Yes, they are stacked in packages at the back of this warehouse that I am using. I don't know where they came from, and I am so very thankful to have someone give them out.

Living four hours away, we could not drive over to get them every time we needed more, and when we checked, we discovered that it would cost $54 for postage to mail one bundle of 250 at a time. So, Daddy and

I prayed and asked God to provide a way to get them over to us if He wanted Daddy to give them out.

God worked out a plan. Here it is: I had helped one of my mother's very good friends, Lenna Mae, in her later years. She lived about two miles from where we lived on Couch Mountain. While helping her, I met her brother, Lawrence Rice, who came monthly to visit his sister from his home there in Tennessee. When Daddy and I prayed about how to get the posters to us, Lawrence came to mind. So, I called him and asked if there was a possibility of him swinging by that warehouse and bringing "a few" Ten Commandment posters with him when he came to visit his sister here in North Carolina.

Lawrence was delighted. He said, "I just bought a new SUV, and I was praying that God would give me something to use it for to serve Him. This is it! Thank you for the opportunity!" He was so excited!

So, Lawrence started bringing as many bundles of Ten Commandment posters as he could get in his SUV with whatever else he was bringing to his sister Lenna Mae. Sometimes it was just one or two bundles, and sometimes he was able to bring as many as twelve bundles at a time!

At first, Daddy wanted to give them out door-to-door. So, we covered several neighborhoods. But in his praying one day, Daddy said, "Let's give them to businesses for a gift for their employees." From industries to private businesses, all but one took them and were thrilled to take enough to give one to each of their employees.

Then Daddy said, "Let's see if the area churches would want them for their members." All the different denominations that we went to were thrilled to get them for each of their members. For example, one Presbyterian church took 1,500 for members and to give out for gifts for Vacation Bible School that was coming up in a couple of weeks.

One Baptist church took 3,000 for their members. The pastor said, "We just finished a series of sermons on the Ten Commandments. This will be a perfect gift and reminder to each member of our church to finish off our series" (God's timing is perfect!).

The local Catholic Church took several hundred. Every church denomination that we went to took them and were delighted to get them.

I stopped counting at 25,000, so I don't know an exact amount, but Daddy gave out OVER 25,000 Ten Commandments posters before he died.

Daddy had said when he started this project, pointing to the fourth commandment, "This is getting ready to be the issue, and the people that are not reading their Bibles are not going to know. If they have these Ten Commandments posters hanging on their wall, and read them once in a while, they will at least be able to make an intelligent decision when the test comes to them."

One day, before Daddy even knew about the Ten Commandments posters, on nationwide news, the newscasters were discussing and telling us about all the different state and federal laws and how there were (at that time—there are more now, of course) 6,000 + laws altogether in the United States, so Daddy used that when he was giving out the Ten Commandments posters. He told the people, "The US has over 6,000 laws, and THAT'S JUST ONE COUNTRY! Think how many laws there are in all the countries together. But God rules the WHOLE UNIVERSE with JUST TEN LAWS. If we ALL kept these ten laws, we would not need those 6,000."

Each time, as the people stopped to think about that, they said, "Hey, you're right—WOW!" as they took more and more of the Ten Commandments posters.

God has His people in many churches, many denominations. And now, so close to the end of time, He is calling them out of Babylon (false teachings). Like in His last warning to the world in Revelation 14:6–11, the three angels' messages, and in Revelation 18:1–5, especially verse 4, calling to ALL His people wherever they are in the world. "Babylon ... is fallen" (verse 2). "Come out of her, my people, that ye be not partakers of her sins, and that ye receive not of her plagues" (verse 4).

Then verse 12 of Revelation 14 tells what God's true people will be like when He comes to get them. They will have "the patience of the saints." They will be totally keeping God's law (the Ten Commandments, including the second and fourth commandments), and they will have "the faith of Jesus." Friends, that is the most faith you can have, the faith (trust) that He had here on earth and has in His Father. Isn't that exciting to know that we can have that much faith, too, if we just ask?! So, pray every day for those three things: the patience of the saints, to keep the commandments of God, and have the faith of Jesus.

> *"The US has over 6,000 laws, and THAT'S JUST ONE COUNTRY! Think how many laws there are in all the countries together. But God rules the WHOLE UNIVERSE with JUST TEN LAWS. If we ALL kept these ten laws, we would not need those 6,000."*

Let's each one pray that we will be one of those in the "my people" group that is ready to go home with Jesus when He comes to take us home with Him.

Remember, precious reader friend, for everything God says, Satan has a counterfeit. But God is teaching me that He always means what He says. So, believe in Him and worship Him, no matter what Satan tries to tell us (you and me). Pray that you believe God and keep ALL His Ten Commandments. So, here they are as God wrote them Himself with His own finger.

1. **"Thou shall have no other gods before me"** (Exod. 20:3).

    There are many ways we humans make gods out of things and ideas. It's anything we worship—anything other than God that comes between us and God. For example, I used to think that my ideas were as good as anybody else's ideas—so much so, that they were like a god to me. I put them before God, stubbornly, in order to get them across to other people. But God means what He says, and I am praying that God will help me overcome sin and Satan.

2. **"Thou shalt not make unto thee any graven image, or any likeness of any thing that is in heaven above, or that is in the earth beneath, or that is in the water under the earth. Thou shalt not bow down thyself to them, nor serve them: for I the LORD thy God am a jealous God, visiting the iniquity of the fathers upon the children unto the third and fourth generation of them that hate me; and shewing mercy unto thousands of them that love me, and keep my commandments"** (verses 4–5).

    There are many, many people in our world today that maybe have never read the true second commandment, because they have in their homes and out in their yards, figurines and statues of certain people that they worship. But these precious people do not know that Satan's counterfeit of God's law totally leaves out this second commandment and then splits the tenth commandment into two parts to make it total ten laws. We must pray for all people all the time anyway but also that all will learn God's true whole law and keep it, because God means what He says.

3. **"Thou shalt not take the name of the LORD thy God in vain; for the LORD will not hold him guiltless that taketh his name in vain"** (verse 7).

    Sometimes it seems so innocent to use works like, gee, golly, gosh, oh my god, etc. One that I used for years was, "Oh, my goodness!"

Until one day, my daddy said, "YOU don't have any goodness, only God does." After learning that from Daddy, I started praying about it, and God helped me to quit saying that. Also, claiming to be a Christian when not acting like one is another way to take God's name in vain. God means what He says.

4. **"Remember the sabbath day, to keep it holy. Six days shalt thou labor, and do all thy work: but the seventh day is the sabbath of the LORD thy God: in it thou shalt not do any work, thou, nor thy son, nor thy daughter, thy manservant, nor thy maidservant, nor thy cattle, nor thy stranger that is within thy gates: for in six days the LORD made heaven and earth, the sea, and all that in them is, and rested the seventh day: wherefore, the LORD blessed the sabbath day, and hallowed it."** (verses 8–11).

Many, many people (in fact the majority of the world now) seem to believe that it does not matter what day we keep holy—just so we keep one day holy. But God means what He says. Satan's counterfeits will NOT work. Besides, we cannot keep a day holy that God has not made holy. Also, God says to KEEP it holy, not MAKE it holy. Human beings cannot make a day holy. In creating the seventh-day Sabbath, God showed His creative power. In keeping Sabbath holy, we remember God's redemptive power. "The sabbath was made for man, and not man for the sabbath: therefore, the Son of man is Lord also of the sabbath" (Mark 2:27–28).

> The Sabbath was hallowed at the creation. As ordained for man, it had its origin when 'the morning starts sang together, and all the sons of God shouted for joy.' Job 38:7. Peace brooded over the world; for earth was in harmony with heaven. 'God saw everything that He had made, and, behold, it was very good;' and He rested in the joy of His completed work. Genesis 1:31. Because He had rested upon the Sabbath, 'God blessed the seventh day, and sanctified it,'—set it apart to a holy use. He gave it to Adam as a day of rest. It was a memorial of the work of creation, and thus a sign of God's power and His love. The Scripture says, 'He hath made His wonderful works to be remembered.' 'The things that are made,' declare 'the invisible things of Him since the creation of the world,' 'even His everlasting power and divinity.' (*The Desire of Ages,* p. 281)

> The Sabbath was not for Israel merely, but for the world. It had been made known to man in Eden, and, like the other precepts

of the Decalogue, it is of imperishable obligation. Of that law of which the fourth commandment forms a part, Christ declares, 'Till heaven and earth pass, one jot or one tittle shall in nowise pass from the law.' So long as the heavens and the earth endure, the Sabbath will continue as a sign of the Creator's power. And when Eden shall bloom on earth again, God's holy rest day will be honored by all beneath the sun. 'From one Sabbath to another' the inhabitants of the glorified new earth shall go up 'to worship before Me, saith the Lord.' Matthew 5:18; Isaiah 66:23. (Ibid., p. 283)

'The Sabbath was made for man, and not man for the Sabbath,' Jesus said. The institutions that God has established are for the benefit of mankind. 'All things are for your sakes.' 'Whether Paul, or Apollos, or Cephas, or the world, or life, or death, or things present, or things to come; all are yours; and ye are Christ's; and Christ is God's.' 2 Corinthians 4:15; 1 Corinthians 3:22, 23. The law of Ten Commandments, of which the Sabbath forms a part, God gave to His people as a blessing. 'The Lord commanded us,' said Moses, 'to do all these statutes, to fear the Lord our God, for our good always, that He might preserve us alive.' Deuteronomy 6:24. And through the psalmist the message was given to Israel, 'Serve the Lord with gladness: come before His presence with singing. Know ye that the Lord He is God: it is He that hath made us, and not we ourselves; we are His people, and the sheep of His pasture. Enter into His gates with thanksgiving, and into His courts with praise.' Psalm 100:2-4. And of all who keep 'the Sabbath from polluting it,' the Lord declares, 'Even them will I bring to My holy mountain, and make them joyful in My house of prayer.' Isaiah 56:6, 7. (Ibid., p. 288)

5. **"Honour thy father and thy mother: that thy days may be long upon the land which the LORD thy God giveth thee"** (Exod. 20:12).
Talking back to parents is NOT honoring them. Disobeying parents is NOT honoring them. Taking care of them in their old age IS honoring them. God means what He says. And remember God is our Father.

6. **"Thou shalt not kill"** (verse 13).
We know we should never kill physically, but also talking bad about people and talking against them is killing their reputation. Also withholding help when someone needs it can be a form of killing. Proverbs 3:27 says, "Withhold not good from them to whom it is due, when it is in the power of thine hand to do it." Hate is also

a form of killing/murder. See 1 John 3:15. It reads, "Whosoever hateth his brother is a murderer: and ye know that no murderer hath eternal life abiding in him." God means what He says.

7. **"Thou shalt not commit adultery"** (Exod. 20:14).
Desiring someone who is not your spouse is already adultery—besides the act itself. Jesus said this in Matthew 5:28 which reads, "But I say unto you, That whosoever looketh on a woman to lust after her hath committed adultery with her already in his heart." Remember, it was sexual temptation that Satan used to lead Israel into false worship and sin to bring God's displeasure upon them in Numbers 24 and 25. Also, Paul warns us today against immorality in Hebrews 13:4. God means what He says.

8. **"Thou shalt not steal"** (Exod. 20:15).
Stealing physically is wrong, as we all know. But so is stealing someone's affections or reputation, etc. Satan has many, many counterfeits of God's eighth law too. God means what He says.

9. **"Thou shalt not bear false witness against thy neighbor"** (verse 16).
Any kind of deceit is bearing false witness, including plain lying. Satan hits us with things like "Oh, this one little lie won't matter." Satan says, "Go ahead and say those flattering things to make that person feel better, even though it's not true, but no one will know." White lies, "fish stories," exaggeration, staying silent when you should speak up and correct something, and the intent to deceive are all examples of bearing false witness. Satan is loaded with counterfeits that can seem right at the time but can ruin someone. But God means what He says.

10. **"Thou shalt not covet thy neighbor's house, thou shalt not covet they neighbor's wife, nor his manservant, nor his maidservant, nor his ox, nor his ass, nor any thing that is thy neighbor's"** (verse 17).
"Wow, I sure wish I had his car; it is so cool!" "Man, I would love to have her husband; he is so kind to me." In our thoughts is where it starts. It leads to stealing and breaking God's other laws. Covetousness also includes greediness: wanting more than you have at the time. "For this ye know, that no whoremonger, nor unclean person, *nor covetous man, who is an idolater*, hath any inheritance in the kingdom of Christ and of God" (Eph. 5:5, emphasis mine). God means what He says.

If we live up to the knowledge that we have, we will receive greater knowledge. We are held accountable for what we know and what we have opportunity to learn. So maybe some people who have not had the opportunity to learn God's law will only be held accountable for what they had opportunity to learn.

"Therefore to him that knoweth to do good, and doeth it not, to him it is sin" (James 4:17). And "For whosoever shall keep the whole law, and yet offend in one point, he is guilty of all" (James 2:10).

Holiness is not the way to Jesus, but Jesus is the way to holiness. And we show God we love Him by keeping His law (commandments). He himself says, "If ye love me, keep my commandments" (John 14:15). The first four commandments show our love to God. The last six show our duty to our fellow man. Jesus summed it up Himself in Mark 12:30–31. "And thou shalt love the Lord thy God with all thy heart, and with all thy soul, and with all thy mind, and with all thy strength.... Thou shall love thy neighbor as thyself."

I heard one speaker say it this way: "Jesus died without our request and was raised without our request. That is His part—our part is to choose." Let's pray every day that God will help us choose Him and that God will keep us from being deceived with all of Satan's counterfeits and that God will lead us into ALL TRUTH so we will be ready for Jesus' second coming.

The Bible Stands

Haldor Lillenas, 1917

Public Domain
Courtesy of the Cyber Hymnal™

The Return

Speaking of Christ's second coming, maybe you, dear reader friend, would like to read some of the Bible verses telling how this most beautiful event is going to happen. I have been trying to memorize these verses myself so I will not be deceived on this point. Because guess what? Satan is going to try to counterfeit this event too. One main difference is that Satan, after his "grand entry" to this world as an angel of light, will be walking around on earth lying and deceiving people, claiming to be Christ and saying that he has changed the seventh-day Sabbath to Sunday and any other counterfeits that he can get people to believe.

Remember, God NEVER CHANGES. "I change not" (Mal. 3:6). Our God in heaven is not going to change HIS law or anything that HE has already told us in HIS Word, the Bible.

But when Jesus comes, He will not touch this sinful world, but His people will be brought up to HIM in the air by His angels.

Oh my! I'm getting ahead of the story. Let's see what the Bible says about this most exciting event. The Bible speaks of this wonderful, awesome, exciting event (His return to earth to receive His people that love Him) more than 1,500 times. Here are some of the Bible texts telling this:

1. What does Jesus promise? John 14:1–3 (notice especially verse 3): "Let not your heart be troubled: ye believe in God, believe also in me. In my Father's house are many mansions: if it were not so, I would have told you. I go to prepare a place for you. And if I go and prepare a place for you, I will come again, and receive you unto myself; that where I am, there ye may be also."

2. When will Jesus come? The disciples asked Him in Matthew 24:3: "Tell us, when shall these things be? and what shall be the sign of thy coming, and of the end of the world?"

3. Jesus made it clear that He could not give an exact date. Matthew 24:36 reads, "But of that day and hour knoweth no man, no, not the angels of heaven, but my Father only."

4. But Jesus answered His disciples' question by telling them of signs, or mileposts, they could observe to know that history was and now is moving toward the great climax of ALL time—the second coming of Christ. Let's look at some of these signs that Jesus told His disciples to look for. Signs in the physical world: Matthew 24:7 (second part), "[A]nd there shall be famines, and pestilences [illness, disease], and earthquakes, in divers [various] places." NOTE: Over 1.2 billion people on our planet cannot afford the basic necessities of food, clothing, and shelter (Andrea Peer, "Global poverty: Facts, FAQs, and how to help," World Vision, https://www.worldvision.org/sponsorship-news-stories/global-poverty-facts [last modified April 4, 2023]). Famine and earthquakes are another sign.

5. Signs in the political world: Matthew 24:6–7, "And ye shall hear of wars and rumours of wars: see that ye be not troubled: for all these things must come to pass, but the end is not yet. For nation shall rise against nation, and kingdom against kingdom." When you hear the daily news, you can see that the world governments are in constant struggle with each other, which is another sign of the end of time.

6. Signs in the intellectual world: Daniel is an Old Testament prophet who was given information by God about the time of the end. What did he say about it? Daniel 12:4 reads, "But thou, O Daniel, shut up the words, and seal the book, even to the time of the end: many shall run to and fro, and knowledge shall be increased." Daniel mentioned two things that would earmark the end of time: people hurrying about and an increase in knowledge. Two types of increases will be an (a) increase of knowledge concerning the long-hidden prophecies of Daniel which point to Christ's second coming and (b) an increase in general knowledge and travel. For example, horseback riding to space travel in 100 years and the information overload we have these days. Look at all the computer and Internet usage these days with even little children using their phones to search the Internet.

7. Signs in the social world (sounds like this was just written yesterday instead of 2,500 years ago). 2 Timothy 3:1–5 describes people in the last days: "This know also, that in the last days perilous [dangerous] times shall come. For men shall be lovers of their own selves, covetous, boasters, proud, blasphemers, disobedient to parents,

unthankful, unholy, without natural affection, trucebreakers, false accusers, incontinent, fierce, despisers of those that are good, traitors, heady, high-minded, lovers of pleasures more than lovers of God; having a form of godliness, but denying the power thereof: from such turn away."

8. Signs in the religious world: Jesus warned about a deception that would take place prior to His second coming. What is the deception? Matthew 24:4–5 and 23–24 says, "And Jesus answered and said unto them, Take heed that no man deceive you. For many shall come in my name, saying, I am Christ; and shall deceive many.... Then if any man shall say unto you, Lo, here is Christ, or there; believe it not. For there shall arise false Christs, and false prophets, and shall shew great signs and wonders; insomuch that, if it were possible, they shall deceive the very elect."

9. What do these false Christs and false prophets teach? Matthew 24:23 and 26 reads, "Then if any man shall say unto you, Lo, here is Christ, or there; believe it not.... Wherefore if they shall say unto you, Behold, he is in the desert; go not forth: behold, he is in the secret chambers; believe it not." Today there are many people who teach that Jesus is coming secretly or that He has already come.

10. What did Jesus say you should do when you hear these teachings? In Matthew 24:26 the last part, Jesus says, "BELIEVE IT NOT."

11. Why? Matthew 24:27–30: "For as the lightning cometh out of the east, and shineth even unto the west; so shall also the coming of the Son of man be. For wheresoever the carcase is, there will the eagles be gathered together. Immediately after the tribulation of those days shall the sun be darkened, and the moon shall not give her light, and the stars shall fall from heaven, and the powers of the heavens shall be shaken: And then shall appear the sign of the Son of man in heaven: and then shall all the tribes of the earth mourn, and they shall see the Son of man coming in the clouds of heaven with power and great glory." Revelation 1:7 also says, "Behold, he cometh with clouds; and every eye shall see him, and they also which pierced him: and all kindreds of the earth shall wail because of him. Even so, Amen." Jesus describes His coming not as an obscure happening but as an event that will demand the attention of the whole world because of its glory and power. "Every eye shall see him." Look at all the signs Christ gave His

disciples in Matthew 24; they all lead to His coming, but the end is not yet. Matthew 24:6, the last part, reads "[F]or all these things must come to pass; but the end is not yet." But there is one sign that Jesus said that once it was accomplished, then He <u>would</u> come. What is it?

12. Jesus will come after this sign: Matthew 24:14 says, "And this gospel of the kingdom shall be preached in all the world for a witness unto all nations; and then shall the end come." You can measure the nearness of Christ's second coming by the progress of the gospel proclamation to the world. This is why the early Christians spread the gospel everywhere. They wanted Jesus to come soon. But during the Dark Ages, this emphasis became obscured. Then in the last century, as Christians focused once again on the Bible message of the second coming of Christ, they were stirred to tell the world about it! Mission programs sprang up all over the world. Today, there are thousands of dedicated Christians carrying the gospel of Christ to every part of the globe. God has a thousand ways to accomplish His work. Who knows how swiftly He could finish the distribution of the gospel story?

Also, as you have probably realized by now, these Bible prophecies are being fulfilled even faster today than ever before right before our very eyes.

Natural disasters including hurricanes, typhoons, cyclones (depending on what part of the world you are in), tornadoes, earthquakes, and forest fires are now more frequent and more intense than they have ever been before. Along with this is the increasing unrest of attitudes and contentions of the people throughout the whole world today, like it says in 2 Timothy 3:1–5 (see number 7). This description of the people of the world written way back then could easily be headlines now in our newspaper and media news reports today.

Isn't it exciting, dear reader? It's truly almost time for Jesus to return! The devastation that is happening is terrible, but the fact that it is pointing to Christ's second coming to earth very soon now is so very exciting! We should be praying more now than we have ever prayed before. Pray that we will not be deceived by all these counterfeits and that we will be ready for Christ's second coming.

Pray that we will be like Jesus, a blessing to everyone we meet. In E.G. White's *The Desire of Ages*, page 70, it says that "He [Jesus] lived to bless others." We want to be like Jesus so we can pray, "Help me to be like Jesus, a blessing to all with whom I come in contact." And pray that we—you and me—will TOTALLY reflect God's character.

So, we can each also pray that we will totally reflect God's character, like it says in E.G. White's *Christ's Object Lessons* on page 69:

> When the character of Christ shall be perfectly reproduced in His people, then He will come to claim them as His own. It is the privilege of every Christian not only to look for but to hasten the coming of our Lord Jesus Christ, (2 Peter 3:12). Were all who profess His name bearing fruit to His glory, how quickly the whole world would be sown with the seed of the gospel. Quickly the last great harvest would be ripened, and Christ would come to gather the precious grain.

Thankfully, Christ's return to this earth the second time is going to put an end to all our suffering, stress, sickness, and all crime, destruction, and sin. PRAISE GOD!

Thankfully, Christ's return to this earth the second time is going to put an end to all our suffering, stress, sickness, and all crime, destruction, and sin. PRAISE GOD!

Keep looking up, dear reader friend. Jesus is coming soon!

Jesus Is Coming Again

Jessie E. Strout, 1872

George E. Lee

Public Domain
Courtesy of the Cyber Hymnal™

The Power of Our Awesome God

This story began the day *after* I turned in the manuscript (*God in My Life*, volume 3) to my publisher; hence this story is the last one in the book. (Thank you, Pastor Mesikt Idechong, for insisting that this story get into this book!)

On August 23, 2022, I was getting ready to go visit my son, Dallas, and his family in Idaho. I had been up all day and most of the night for two days getting my work done and packing for the trip.

The plan was that Atsushi was going to take me to the airport around 5:00 in the morning to catch my 6:55 flight. About 3:30 that morning, I was looking for my passport to put it in my purse.

What?! It was not in its usual place! But where was it?

Katy, my daughter, and I looked "high and low" and everywhere we could think of--but no passport. Finally, about 4 a.m., Katy called the airline to cancel my flight and told them the reason. The airline company graciously cancelled but put my reservation on hold so I could use it later.

By then, it was time to start our regular day. So we stayed up to get ready for breakfast.

I had not been feeling well for a few hours, but I had rationalized with myself, *Once I get on the plane I can rest, get some sleep, and then I will feel better.*

Instead, at 6 a.m. I was feeling much worse and was walking through the dining room toward the kitchen to tell somebody I didn't feel good when I collapsed in an unconscious heap on the floor.

Atsushi, my urgent care nurse son-in-law, bent down, took my wrist, and felt for a pulse. There was none. Right then, he and my granddaughter, five year old Lumina, knelt down right there beside me and started praying to our loving God in heaven.

Meanwhile, across the room, Katy was calling 911. After their prayer, Atsushi again took my pulse. He started feeling a slow, very faint heart beat starting up again. I regained consciousness enough to talk a little bit.

The ambulance arrived, and I ended up in the hospital emergency room instead of at the airport. There, God even provided a person I knew to encourage me. A friend came up beside my stretcher and said, "Rita, this is Ron. I am praying for you."

I was still in the emergency room the next day when my heart stopped again. God used the professional staff to bring me back to life again. This time, while God was bringing me back to life, He brought the pool of Bethesda to my mind—the story of the man that had a disease for thirty-eight years lying on his mat unable to walk, with no one to help him into the pool. This Bible story is found in John 5:2–9. Jesus walked up to him and said, "Wilt thou be made whole?"

The man, in essence, said, "Yes, but there's no one to help me!"

Jesus told him, "Rise, take up thy bed, and walk." Instantly the man jumped to his feet, rolled up his bed and walked. He was healed!

Right then God said to me, "*I Am* the same God that is with you." That was so beautiful and encouraging. I had no fear. At the very same time that God was bringing me back to life, He gave me a very strong impression of urgency—an urgency to **hurry** to get ready for something.

Then I was taken to the intensive care unit (ICU) and was there for a few days before being transferred to the cardiac unit. The day after that, I was taken for a minimally invasive heart procedure. After that, the technicians took me back to my room for recovery. Just as they got me into my room, my heart stopped again.

God brought me back to life again. This time while I was "coming back," God showed me the miracle in Daniel 3: The Hebrews in the fiery furnace with Jesus walking around in there with them, and only the ropes that bound them were burned off. The three Hebrew men themselves came walking out of the fire with no burns or no smell of smoke on them. Right then, God gave me another reassurance. "*I Am* the same God taking care of you." Again I had no fear, knowing God was with me. At the same time, an even stronger urgency came to me saying, "**Hurry!** He's coming!"

I was taken back to ICU. The next day, while still in ICU, my heart stopped again for the fourth time. This time, the nurse told Katy it stopped for over seven seconds. (We were not told the lengths of any previous episodes—what they call a "code blue" in the hospital). We surely serve an awesome God! He saved my life four times in two weeks.

As God was bringing me back to life this fourth time, He gave me another exciting and peaceful reassurance. I saw a place in the sky open up and I was allowed to see Jesus standing on the right hand of God, His Father (and our Father). Jesus was asking God to be able to come and get us, as He says in John 17:24, "Father, I will that they also, whom thou hast given me, be with me where I am...."

Honestly, I cannot think of any human words to describe the joy and peace of that beautiful scene and what it meant to me then and what it still means to me now. No words describe it! To know without any doubt that our Jesus is wanting us with Him—that is truly awesome! I can still see that beautiful scene in my memory.

Through all of this, there was even a stronger urgency—**Jesus is coming** *sooner* **now! Be ready!!!**

Just think dear reader, friend, Jesus **wants** to come get us! He loves us—you and me—so much that He wants us with Him. He loves all of us the same.

He wants to get us out of this present world of crime, stress, sickness, discouragement, depression, and death. And He will take us to live with Him in heaven where it's all peace, joy and love. Isn't that so very exciting! I love it!

That's why the Bible tells about Christ's second coming so many times (over 1,500 times like we saw in the previous chapter). He is coming back in the clouds and every eye shall see Him coming (1 Thes. 4:13–18; Rev. 1:7).

Another miracle that God worked out was that, as He brought me back to life each time, He gave me the strength to talk and witness for Him. I was able to give some literature to each and every person who helped me. Doctors, nurses, nursing assistants, plus lab techs, physical therapists, maintenance workers, cafeteria and kitchen workers, housekeeping staff and others.

Katy and Atsushi brought grocery bags full of literature on all types of health subjects, including physical, mental and spiritual (sharing the source of our peace).

God gave me the strength to reach into the bag of literature I had sitting on the side of my bed and give a magazine or book full of hope to each person that helped me.

It was one way I could thank them for all they did for me. They were all so sweet and precious, and so appreciative too. All of them said "thank you," and many of them said things like, "Oh, wow, just what I need!"

God had me give the *Ministry of Healing* book to the head code nurse. She held it, staring at it, then back at me. She said, "I really need this. Today is my last day to work. I am leaving in two days to fly back to the States to see what can be done for me and my health problem. I will read this on the plane. Thank you so much!" That's a book that has all three aspects of health in it: physical, mental, spiritual. God knew what she needed.

There was a dopamine drip going into my veins. They said it was the only thing keeping my heart rate up and therefore keeping me alive.

The doctors and some nurses started talking to me about having a pacemaker put in. They said that was the only way I could live. I didn't know much about a pacemaker. One of my patients got one and died a few hours later. But I wasn't afraid, just didn't know much about them. The next morning I was sitting up in my ICU bed thinking and praying while no one was in there. I prayed, "God do you want me to get a pacemaker?" Very plainly God said back to me, "*I Am* the true Healer of hearts. I do not need a pacemaker to heal your heart." At the same time the medicine drip came to my mind. God's words applied to that also. That was all I needed to know. God has been in my life, saving my life, *all* of my life.

A few minutes after my prayer and God's answer, Katy came into my room. She looked very worried. After we both said "good morning," I told Katy, "God doesn't need a pacemaker to heal my heart."

She looked so relieved as she said, "What makes you say that?" I told her I was praying about it and what God's answer had been. Relieved, she said, "Atsushi and I were just praying before I left home that God would show you and us which way would be best. This is our answer!"

At the same time that I was praying, Katy and Atsushi were praying. And we later learned that at that very same time, 5,700 miles away, Dallas and Susanna were praying about the same thing. All three families were praying about the same situation at the same time and God heard and answered. Don't we serve an awesome God! Isn't that a beautiful example of how intercessory prayer works?!

Though many people did CPR on me, at many different times, none of my ribs were broken or even cracked. I had no pain. My respiratory therapist friend said, "That would be impossible! And it's definitely *several* miracles!"

After God saved my life the fourth time and answered our prayers about the pacemaker, I told the nurse and doctors that I did not want to get a pacemaker and I wanted to get off the medicine drip. Very reluctantly, and with much lecturing that I would die that night or the next morning, the doctors agreed to let me wean off of the medicine drip. They were convinced that I would die that night as they were lowering the dopamine drip and I was not getting the pacemaker.

The drip was as high as it could go and I was told later that when the concentration is that high the patient is usually unconscious. But I was awake and could converse normally as God kept me alert.

The nurse came and lowered it every hour or two. Katy spent the night with me and could see my monitor from her sleeping position. When she woke up at 1:30 a.m., she saw that my heart rate was up in the 120s even though they had been weaning me down for a few hours already. Isn't our God awesome?!

The next day when the drip was completely off, my heart rate stabilized in the 60s to 70s. Don't we serve an awesome God?!

My different doctors told me that I would still die without the pacemaker. They said I was committing suicide. I wanted these very precious and helpful doctors that were so worried about me to understand why I was making this decision. I told them, "If my God in heaven isn't finished with me, all the diseases in the world can't kill me. And if He is through with me, then I can just go to sleep and wait for His second coming when He will come again and wake me up. So don't worry. If it is God's will, either way will be just fine."

Now we can see why I couldn't find my passport that morning to fly to visit my son. God had his hand over my passport to keep me from being somewhere in transit when the first heart attack happened. I might have been boarding the plane or already been on it. Instead, I was with Atsushi and Lumina, and through their prayers God gave life back to me. When I returned home from the hospital, we found the passport easily.

Different doctors, nurses, and physician assistants have told me that in all their years of working in the medical field, they have heard of people "coming back" once, rarely twice but not three times and never four times. They have all said it had to be our loving God in heaven that brought me back to life all those times. Don't we serve an awesome God?!!

As you read this, it has been many months since I left the hospital. God keeps me going. I live moment by moment totally in His care. I praise and thank Him every day.

I take no drugs. To me, after God has miraculously brought me back to life so many times, it makes no sense to take my life out of His hands and place it in dependence on manmade drugs. It seems to me if I did that, I would be telling God that I don't trust Him anymore—like Elijah failed to trust Him, after God worked those miracles for him on Mount Carmel sending fire down from heaven to burn up Elijah's sacrifice in front of those hundreds of people. Then when Queen Jezebel threatened to kill Elijah, he suddenly got scared and ran away, like he did not trust God to take care of him anymore. But of course, God was still taking care of him. God went to where he was hiding and asked, "What are you doing here?" (Read the rest of the story in 1 Kings 19.)

There are so many miracles in this story of my hospital experience, probably some I do not even know yet. One more happened with my hospital bill.

I chose to finally leave the hospital on my own because the doctors would *not* let me go until I let them give me a pacemaker. We parted on good terms, though. I sent thank you notes to all of them after I got home. The head doctor had kept telling me, "I am treating you like I treat my own family." Isn't that so precious! It was *so* sweet of him and I thanked him every time he told me that.

They told me, while I was still in the hospital, that the major insurance company I use would *not* pay if I was not discharged by a doctor. The hospital business office told me the same thing when I checked out; I thanked them for letting me know.

That major insurance company had always paid eighty percent of my bills in the past. Through the next few weeks, my family and I were all praying that God would somehow take care of the bill, and/or show me what to do to pay it.

I left the hospital in September. Three months later, in December, I received notification from my insurance company that not only did they pay the eighty percent, but they paid the whole bill—over $104,000! You know that had to be our God in heaven that worked that out. Don't we serve an awesome God?!!

Truthfully, you could say that we are all living moment by moment. None of us really know which moment will be our last. But we *can* know that Jesus loves us dearly and wants us to love Him enough to obey Him.

Dear reader, friend, if you have not yet given your heart to Jesus, please, please, talk to Him right now! Ask Him to forgive your sins and to abide in you and help you to abide in Him.

I always pray for you, dear reader. I pray that whoever reads these books will see God in their lives too, and come to Him before it's too late!

If we all *do* give our hearts to Him, we will get to meet each other and be together in heaven with our Jesus who made it all possible!

Isn't that exciting and wonderful?!

Don't we serve an awesome God?!!

Epilogue

The Lord will not leave His afflicted, tried children to be the sport of Satan's temptations. It is your privilege to trust in Jesus. The heavens are full of rich blessings.... We have not because we ask not, or because we do not pray in faith, believing that we shall be blessed with the special influence of the Holy Spirit. To the true seeker through the mediation of Christ the gracious influences of the Holy Spirit are imparted. (*That I May Know Him,* p. 78)

All who are pursuing the onward Christian course should have, and will have, an experience that is living, that is new and interesting. A living experience is made up of daily trials, conflicts, and temptations, strong efforts and victories, and great peace and joy gained through Jesus. A simple relation of such experiences gives light, strength, and knowledge that will aid others in their advancement in the divine life. The worship of God should be both interesting and instructive to those who have any love for divine and heavenly things. (*Testimonies for the Church*, vol. 2, p. 579)

That's why these books have been written, and it is my prayer that they relate experiences that will "aid others in their advancement in the divine life."

Hold the Fort

That which ye have already hold fast till I come. Rev. 2:25
Behold, I come quickly: hold that fast which thou hast, that no man take thy crown. 3:11

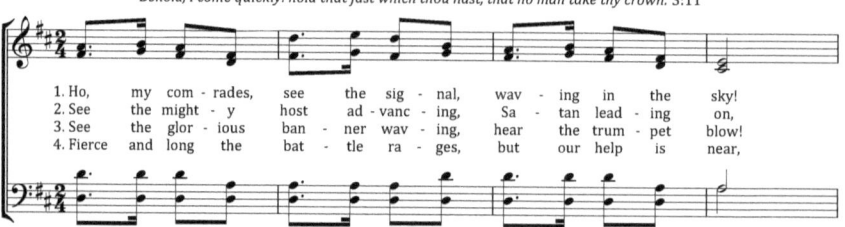

1. Ho, my com-rades, see the sig-nal, wav-ing in the sky!
2. See the might-y host ad-vanc-ing, Sa-tan lead-ing on,
3. See the glor-ious ban-ner wav-ing, hear the trum-pet blow!
4. Fierce and long the bat-tle ra-ges, but our help is near,

Re - in-force-ments now ap-pear-ing, vic-to-ry is nigh.
Might-y ones a-round us fall-ing, cour-age al-most gone!
In our Lead-er's Name we'll tri-umph o-ver eve-ry foe.
On-ward comes our great Com-mand-er, cheer, my com-rades, cheer!

Refrain

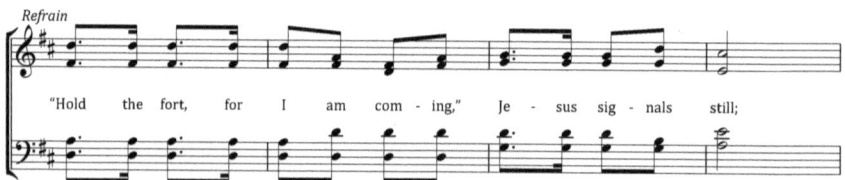

"Hold the fort, for I am com-ing," Je-sus sig-nals still;

Wave the an-swer back to heav-en, "By Thy grace we will."

WORDS and MUSIC: Philip P. Bliss, 1870. Public Domain.

Bibliography

Atsushy04. "Fomentations." YouTube. https://1ref.us/rrgl1 (uploaded May 19, 2020).

Atsushy04. "Hydrotherapy Hot Foot Bath." YouTube. https://1ref.us/244 (uploaded May 19, 2020).

CitizenoftheRealm. "The Wonders of Water." YouTube. https://1ref.us/245 (uploaded January 8, 2014).

Peer, Andrea. "Global poverty: Facts, FAQs, and how to help." World Vision. https://1ref.us/rrgl2 (last modified April 4, 2023).

White, Ellen G. *Christ's Object Lessons.* Washington, DC: Review and Herald, 1900.

———. *Last Day Events.* Boise, ID: Pacific Press, 1992.

———. *Patriarchs and Prophets.* Mountain View, CA: Pacific Press, 1890.

———. *Selected Messages*. Book 2. Washington, DC: Review and Herald, 1958

———. *Selected Messages*. Book 3. Washington, DC: Review and Herald, 1980.

———. *Sons and Daughters of God.* Washington, DC: Review and Herald, 1955.

———. *Steps to Christ.* Mountain View, CA: Pacific Press, 1892.

———. *Testimonies for the Church*. Vol. 2. Mountain View, CA: Pacific Press, 1871.

———. *Testimonies for the Church Containing Messages of Warning and Instruction to Seventh-day Adventists.* 1906.

———. *That I May Know Him.* Washington, DC: Review and Herald, 1964.

———. *The Desire of Ages.* Mountain View, CA: Pacific Press, 1898.

———. *This Day With God*. Washington, DC: Review and Herald, 1979.

TEACH Services, Inc.
PUBLISHING

We invite you to view the complete
selection of titles we publish at:
www.TEACHServices.com

We encourage you to write us
with your thoughts about this,
or any other book we publish at:
info@TEACHServices.com

TEACH Services' titles may be purchased in
bulk quantities for educational, fund-raising,
business, or promotional use.
bulksales@TEACHServices.com

Finally, if you are interested in seeing
your own book in print, please contact us at:
publishing@TEACHServices.com
We are happy to review your manuscript at no charge.

www.ingramcontent.com/pod-product-compliance
Lightning Source LLC
Chambersburg PA
CBHW040313170426
43195CB00020B/2957